READ & SPEAK

KOREAN

—FOR BEGINNERS—

SECOND EDITION

The Easiest Way to Learn to Communicate Right Away!

Series Concept
Jane Wightwick

Korean Edition
Sunjeong Shin

Mc
Graw
Hill

New York Chicago San Francisco Lisbon London Madrid Mexico City
Milan New Delhi San Juan Seoul Singapore Sydney Toronto

The McGraw·Hill Companies

Copyright © 2011 by g-and-w Publishing. All rights reserved. Printed in the United States of America. Except as permitted under the United States Copyright Act of 1976, no part of this publication may be reproduced or distributed in any form or by any means, or stored in a database or retrieval system, without the prior written permission of the publisher.

1 2 3 4 5 6 7 8 9 10 11 12 13 14 15 16 17   QDB/QDB   1 9 8 7 6 5 4 3 2 1

ISBN 978-0-07-176871-9 (book and CD package)
MHID   0-07-176871-8 (book and CD package)

ISBN 978-0-07-176870-2 (book)
MHID   0-07-176870-X (book)

Library of Congress Control Number 2010943212

Other titles in this series

Read & Speak Arabic for Beginners, 2nd Ed.
Read & Speak Chinese for Beginners, 2nd Ed.
Read & Speak Greek for Beginners, 2nd Ed.
Read & Speak Japanese for Beginners, 2nd Ed.

Related title

Your First 100 Words in Korean

McGraw-Hill books are available at special quantity discounts to use as premiums and sales promotion, or for use in corporate training programs. To contact a representative, please e-mail us at bulksales@mcgraw-hill.com.

This book is printed on acid-free paper.

Enhanced CD

The accompanying disk contains audio recordings that can be played on a standard CD player. These recordings are also included in MP3 format. For iPod or similar player:

1. Insert the disk into your computer
2. Open the disk via My Computer.
3. Drag the folder "MP3 files_Read & Speak Korean" into the Music Library of iTunes.
4. Sync your iPod with iTunes, then locate the files on your player under: ARTIST › Read & Speak Korean for Beginners, 2nd Ed.

Audio Flashcards

The Key Words vocabularies in this book can be studied online in interactive flashcard format at byki.com./listcentral. Search for "Read and Speak Korean" to locate the lists.

CONTENTS

Read & Speak

PLUS...

- *8 tear-out cards for fun games*

- *Audio CD for listening and speaking practice*

- *Online activities to enhance learning*

INTRODUCTION

Welcome to *Read & Speak Korean*. This program will introduce you to the Korean language in easy-to-follow steps. The focus is on enjoyment and understanding, on reading words rather than writing them yourself. Through activities and games you'll learn how to read and speak basic Korean in less time than you thought possible.

You'll find these features in your program:

	Key Words	See them written and hear them on the CD to improve your pronunciation.
	Language Focus	Clear, simple explanations of language points to help you build up phrases for yourself.
	Activities	Practice what you have learned through reading, listening, and speaking activities.
	Games	With tear-out components. Challenge yourself or play with a friend. A great, fun way to review.
	Audio CD	Hear the key words and phrases and take part in interactive listening and speaking activities. You'll find the track numbers next to the activities in your book.

If you want to give yourself extra confidence with reading the script, you will find *Your First 100 Words in Korean* the ideal pre-course companion to this program. *Your First 100 Words in Korean* introduces the Korean script through 100 key everyday words, many of which also feature in *Read & Speak Korean*.

So now you can take your first steps in Korean with confidence, enjoyment and a real sense of progress.

1

Whenever you see the audio CD symbol, you'll find listening and speaking activities on the CD included with this book. The symbol shows the track number.

Track 1 is an introduction to the sounds of Korean. Listen to this before you start and come back to it again at later stages if you need to.

Key Words

2

Look at the script for each key word and try to visualize it, connecting its image to the pronunciation you hear on your CD.

안녕하세요
annyeong-haseyo
hello

저는 jeoneun
I

이에요 **-ieyo**
am/are/is

안녕히 가세요
annyeong-hi gaseyo
goodbye ("go in peace," said to someone leaving)

안녕히 계세요
annyeong-hi gyeseyo
goodbye ("stay in peace," said to someone staying)

Korean names:

이수진
i-sujin
Sujin Lee (female)

김민준
gim-minjun
Minjun Kim (male)

최영철
choe-yeongcheol
Yeongcheol Choi (male)

박진희
bak-jinhi
Jinhi Park (female)

The Korean "*Hangeul*" script is very logical – words are generally written as they sound. The Hangeul alphabet consists of consonants and vowels which combine to make syllables. The letters that make up an individual syllable are written together in a square shape. All words in Korean are composed of one or more syllables. The pronunciation is shown in the official romanization system.

You will find an overview of the script and the pronunciation in the reference section on page 89, but don't expect to take it all in at once. Concentrate only on some of the more recognisable syllables you meet in the Key Words for the moment and build up gradually from there. Look carefully at the script while listening to the CD, connecting the image to the pronunciation you hear.

How do you say it?

Join the script to the pronunciation, as in the example.

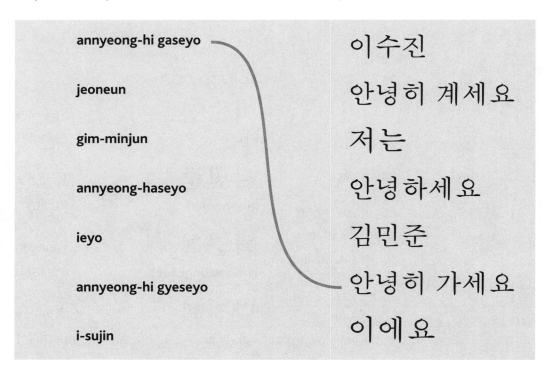

annyeong-hi gaseyo	이수진
jeoneun	안녕히 계세요
gim-minjun	저는
annyeong-haseyo	안녕하세요
ieyo	김민준
annyeong-hi gyeseyo	안녕히 가세요
i-sujin	이에요

What does it mean?

Now say the Korean out loud and write the English next to each.

안녕하세요 _hello_   이에요 _____

김민준 _____   이수진 _____

안녕히 계세요
_____   저는 _____

Language Focus

To introduce yourself you can say 저는 … 이에요 **jeoneun … -ieyo**
(I am …) with your name in the middle.

> 저는 최영철이에요.
> **jeoneun choe-yeongcheol-ieyo** *I am Yeongcheol Choi.*
>
> 저는 마이클이에요.
> **jeoneun maikeul-ieyo** *I am Michael.*

저는 **jeoneun** is made up of the word for *I* – 저 **jeo** – followed by 는 **neun**, a particle which shows that word before is the subject of the sentence. 는 **neun** doesn't have a direct translation, but means something like "*as for.*" 이에요 **-ieyo** is a verb ending that comes after the name and here means *am*. So the Korean sentence actually reads "*I (as for) Michael am.*"

In Korean, honorific words and verb endings exist to express politeness. They are derived from social structure. For example, people who are younger or lower in status show respect for the older or superior person. There are three tiers in verb ending usage: plain form, polite form and honorific form. You cannot use the honorific form when you talk about yourself. 이에요 **-ieyo** is a polite ending. You can also use another, more formal, polite ending, 입니다 **-imnida**, for example, 저는 마이클입니다 **jeoneun maikeul-imnida** *(I am Michael)*.

When you address someone directly, you need to add a title 씨 **-ssi** *(Miss/Ms./Mr./Mrs.)* to the end of the name.

> 안녕하세요, 영철씨.
> **annyung-haseyo, yeongcheol-ssi** *Hello, Yeongcheol.*

Practice introducing yourself
and learn some useful replies
on your CD.

3

What are they saying?

Write the correct number in the word balloons.

1 안녕하세요. 저는 이수진이에요.
annyung-haseyo. jeoneun i-sujin-ieyo

2 안녕하세요, 영철씨.
annyung-haseyo, yeongcheol-ssi

3 안녕히 가세요. **annyeong-hi gaseyo**

4 안녕하세요, 진희씨.
annyung-haseyo, jinhi-ssi

What do you hear?

Work out the phrases below. Then listen and check (✔)
the two phrases you hear on your audio CD.

4

1 안녕하세요. ☐

2 안녕히 가세요, 진희씨. ☐

3 저는 이수진이에요. ☐

4 안녕하세요, 수진씨. ☐

5 안녕히 가세요, 영철씨. ☐

5

Key Words

이름 ireum	*name*
뭐? mwo?	*what?*
이름이 뭐예요? ireum-i mwo-yeyo?	*what's your name?*
고맙습니다 gomap-seumnida	*thank you*
천만에요 cheonman-eyo	*you're welcome*

🔍 Language Focus

The question **What's your name?** is formed as follows: 이름 ireum *(name)* + 이 -i *(subject particle)* + 뭐 mwo *(what)* + 예요 -yeyo *(verb ending "is")*, literally *"name (as for) what is?."* The same question would be used for **What's his name?**, or **What's her name?**. The context will make it clear.

Koreans will give their family name before the first name, for example, 저는 김영순이에요 **jeoneun gim-yeongsun-ieyo**. *I'm Yeongsun Kim*. Here 김 **gim** is the family name and 영순 **yeongsun** is the first name.

이름이 뭐예요?
ireumi mwo-yeyo? *What's your name?*

저는 정지현이에요.
jeoneun jeong-jihyeon-ieyo. *I'm Jihyeon Jeong.*

You can omit 저는 **jeoneun**: 정지현이에요. **jeong-jihyeon-ieyo** *(I) am Jihyeon Jeong*; 제인이에요. **jane-ieyo** *(I) am Jane.*

Speaking practice

Practice the Korean you have learned so far.

6

What does it mean?

Match the English word balloons to the Korean.

For example: **1b**

1 You're welcome.

2 Hello.

3 What's your name?

4 Goodbye .

5 I'm Hyejeong.

6 Thank you.

a 저는 혜정이에요.

b 천만에요.

c 안녕하세요.

d 고맙습니다.

e 이름이 뭐예요?

f 안녕히계세요.

Which word?

Write the correct number of the word in the box
to complete the conversation, as in the example.

1 이에요   **2** 하세요

3 뭐예요   **4** 저는

5 안녕

안녕 __2__.

_____ 하세요.

_____ 최 진만이에요. 이름이 _____?

김수정 _____.

Language Focus

Most Korean names are made up of a single-syllable family name with a double-syllable first name, although occasionally you will find double-syllable surnames, and single- or triple-syllable first names.

Foreign names are phonetically represented so they may sound slightly different. This is particularly noticeable if a name ends with a consonant (except *n, m, r* or *l*). Koreans tend to pronounce the last consonant of the name separately by adding a vowel sound **eu** or **i**, for example, 제크 **jekeu** *(Jack)*, 라지 **laji** *(Raj)*,

Some English sounds that do not exist in Korean, such as *f, th, v,* and *z,* are pronounced as their nearest Korean equivalents (**p, ss, b** and **j**), for example, 제프 **jepeu** *(Geoff)*, 데이비드 **deibideu** *(David)*.

What are their names?

Can you work out these common English names in Korean script?
Use the script tables on pages 89–90 to help you work them out.

사라	*sara Sarah*	팀	_____
헨렌	_____	켄	_____
메리	_____	마크	_____
리사	_____	로버트	_____

In or out?

Who is in the office today and who is out at meetings? Look at the wallchart and write the names in English in the correct column, as in the example.

사라	✔
수진	✔
라지	✘
팀	✔
마이클	✘
헬렌	✘
민준	✔
영철	✔
로버트	✘
진희	✘

IN

Sarah

OUT

The Name Game

(1) Tear out Game Card 1 at the back of your book and cut out the name cards (leave the sentence-build cards at the bottom of the sheet for the moment).

(2) Put the cards Korean side up and see if you can recognize the names. Turn over the cards to see if you were correct.

(3) Keep shuffling the cards and testing yourself until you can read all the names.

(4) Then cut out the extra sentence-build cards at the bottom of the sheet and make mini-dialogs. For example:

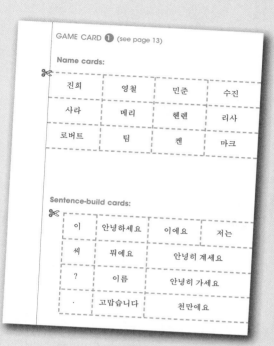

GAME CARD ❶ (see page 13)

Name cards:

진희	영철	민준	수진
사라	메리	헬렌	리사
로버트	팀	켄	마크

Sentence-build cards:

이	안녕하세요	이에요	저는
씨	뭐예요	안녕히 계세요	
?	이름	안녕히 가세요	
.	고맙습니다	천만에요	

| 안녕하세요 | . | 이름 | 이 | 뭐예요 | ? |

| 저는 | 팀 | 이에요 | . |

– **annyeong-haseyo. ireumi mwo-yeyo?**

– **jeoneun tim-ieyo.**

진희   Jinhi

팀   Tim

(5) You can also play with a friend. Make mini-dialogs for each other to read. If you both have a book, you can play Pairs (pelmanism) with both sets of sentence-build cards, saying the words as you turn over the cards.

Key Words

	한국 han-guk	Korea		영국 yeong-guk	England
	중국 jung-guk	China		캐나다 cae-nada	Canada
	일본 ilbon	Japan		아일랜드 ail-landeu	Ireland
	미국 miguk	America		호주 hoju	Australia
	나라 nara	country		도시 dosi	city

Some names of countries end with the syllable 국 **guk** meaning *"country"* (although the word by itself actually means *"soup"*!) Other countries and cities are written phonetically in most cases.

To learn new words, try covering the English and looking at the Korean script and pronunciation. Start from the first word and work your way to the last word seeing if you can remember the English. Then do the same but this time starting from the bottom and moving up to the first word. See if you can go down and up three times without making any mistakes. Then try looking only at the Korean characters and see if you can remember the pronunciation and meaning. When you can recognize all the words, cover the Korean and this time look at the English saying the Korean out loud.

Where are the countries?

Write the number next to the country, as in the example.

캐나다 _1_   아일랜드 __   영국 __   중국 __

일본 __   한국 __   호주 __   미국 __

How do you say it?

Join the English to the pronunciation and the Korean script, as in the example.

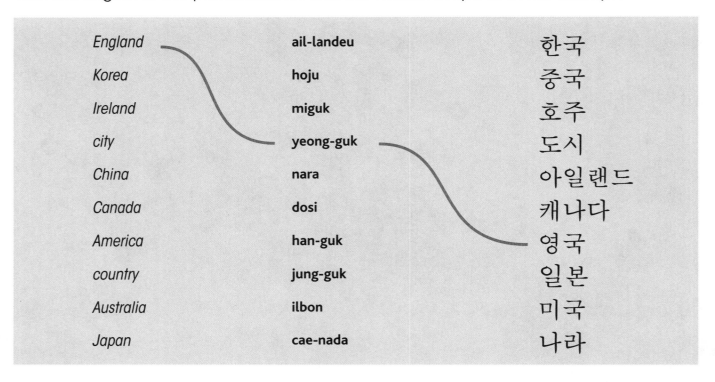

English	pronunciation	Korean
England	ail-landeu	한국
Korea	hoju	중국
Ireland	miguk	호주
city	yeong-guk	도시
China	nara	아일랜드
Canada	dosi	캐나다
America	han-guk	영국
country	jung-guk	일본
Australia	ilbon	미국
Japan	cae-nada	나라

Which city?

See if you can figure out the cities using the English in the box to help you.

Seoul	New York	Washington	Los Angeles
Busan	Sydney	London	

런던   _London_   서울   _____

부산   _____   로스 엔젤레스   _____

시드니   _____   뉴욕   _____

워싱턴   _____

Language Focus

To form a nationality, Korean adds 사람 **saram**, meaning *person* or *people*, to the name of the country. So 한국사람 **hanguk-saram** means *Korean (person/people)*, 영국사람 **yeongguk-saram** means *English (person/people)*, etc. To form sentences, use the verb ending 이에요 **-ieyo** that you learned in Topic 1.

> 저는 중국사람이에요.
> **jeoneun jungguk-saram-ieyo** *I'm Chinese.*
>
> 저는 미국사람이에요.
> **jeoneun miguk-saram-ieyo** *I'm American.*

To say where you come from use the expression 저는 ...에서 왔어요 **jeoneun ...eseo wasseoyo** *(I'm from...)*. 에서 **eseo** is an ending with a meaning similar to the English *from*, and 왔어요 **wasseoyo** means *came*. By adding the name of a city or a country before **eseo** you can say where you are from. If you want to mention both the country and the city you are from, you simply say the name of the city directly after the country.

> 저는 한국에서 왔어요.
> **jeoneun hanguk-eseo wasseoyo** *I come from Korea.*
>
> 저는 뉴욕에서 왔어요.
> **jeoneun nyu-yok-eseo wasseoyo** *I come from New York.*
>
> 저는 호주시드니에서 왔어요
> **jeoneun hoju sideuni-eseo wasseoyo** *I come from Sydney (in) Australia.*

To ask where someone is from, use the question word 어디? **eodi** *(where?)* together with 에서 왔어요 **eseo wasseoyo**:

> 어디에서 왔어요?
> **eodi-eseo wasseoyo?** *Where do you come from?*

8

Listen to six different people introducing themselves and see if you can understand where they are from.

Where are they from?

Join the people to their nationalities, as in the example. Listen again to track 8 on your CD and look back at the names and countries if you need to remind yourself.

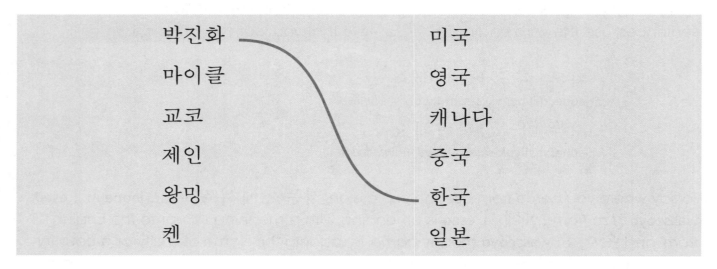

박진화	미국
마이클	영국
교코	캐나다
제인	중국
왕밍	한국
켄	일본

Where are you from?

Now say where you're from.
Follow the prompts on your audio CD.

9

 **Key Words**

10

사람 **saram**	*person/people*	어디에서 왔어요? **eodi-eseo wasseoyo**	*Where do you come from?*
에서 **eseo**	*from*	저는...에서 왔어요 **jeoneun ...-eseo wasseoyo**	*I come from ...*
어디 **eodi**	*where?*		

🔍 *Language Focus*

English often refers to other people as *he* or *she*: *He is American, She is from New York,* etc. Korean speakers rarely use *he* or *she*. Instead they prefer to use the person's name followed by the title 씨 *-ssi (Miss/Ms./Mr./Mrs.)*.

수진씨는 한국에서 왔어요.
sujinssi-neun hanguk-eseo wasseoyo
Sujin comes from Korea.

제인씨는 영국사람이에요.
jeinssi-neun yeongguk-saram-ieyo
Jane is English.

Generally, you can omit pronouns such as *I, you, he* or *she* altogther in Korean if the context is clear.

캐나다에서 왔어요.
caenada-eseo wasseoyo
(I) come from Canada.

어디에서 왔어요?
eodi-eseo wasseoyo?
Where do (you) come from?

중국사람이에요?
jungguksaram-ieyo?
Are (you) Chinese?

Notice from the last example that you can turn a statement into a question in Korean by simply using a questioning tone at the end.

Who's from where?

Make questions and answers about where these people are from, as in the example.

1

피터 piteo

피터씨는 어디에서 왔어요?

piteossi-neun eodi-eseo wasseoyo?

Where does Peter come from?

피터씨는 미국 뉴욕에서 왔어요.

piteossi-neun miguk nyuyok-eseo wasseoyo.

Peter comes from New York (in) America.

2

교코 kyoko

3

헨렌 helen

4

마크 makeu

5

메리 meri

6

수진 sujin

7

왕밍
wangming

8

팀 tim

Listen and check

Listen to the conversation on your audio CD and decide if these sentences are true or false.

		True	False
1	The woman's name is Sophie.	☐	☐
2	She comes from Canada.	☐	☐
3	The man's name is Yeongcheol.	☐	☐
4	He comes from Seoul.	☐	☐
5	They are already friends.	☐	☐

What does it mean?

Now read the Korean you heard in the conversation and match it with the English, as in the example.

I'm Lucy.	저는 캐나다사람이에요.
Pleased to meet you.	한국 부산에서 왔어요.
Hello.	저는 루시예요.
I'm Canadian.	이름이 뭐예요?
What's your name?	안녕하세요.
I come from Busan in Korea.	만나서 반갑습니다.

What does it mean?

Try to work out each of these sentences. It will help if you break them up into the separate words and phrases. Look back at the Key Word panels if you need help.

Then read the sentences out loud when you have figured them out and write the English next to each, as in the example.

1 저는 루시예요.   _I'm Lucy_

2 저는 캐나다사람이에요.   _____

3 수진씨는 한국사람이에요.   _____

4 이름이 뭐예요?   _____

5 저는 박진희예요.   _____

6 팀씨는 어디에서 왔어요?   _____

7 팀씨는 영국에서 왔어요.   _____

8 헨렌씨는 미국에서 왔어요.   _____

You can compare your pronunciation of the sentences with the models on your audio CD.

12

Now complete this description of yourself. Read the sentences out loud, adding your own details.

저는 ...이에요.

저는 ... ...에서 왔어요.

The Flag Game

1. Tear out Game Card 2.

2. Find a die and counter(s).

3. Put the counter(s) on START.

4. Throw the die and move that number of squares.

5. When you land on a flag, you must ask and answer the appropriate question for that country. For example:

어디에서 왔어요?
eodi-eseo wasseoyo?
Where do you come from?

캐나다에서 왔어요.
caenada-eseo wasseoyo
I come from Canada.

6. If you can't remember the question or answer, you must go back to the square you came from. You must throw the exact number to finish.

7. You can challenge yourself or play with a friend.

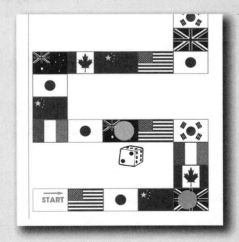

Key Words

의자 **uija**	*chair*	문 **mun**	*door*
탁자 **takja**	*table*	창문 **changmun**	*window*
텔레비전 **telle-bijeon**	*television*	펜 **pen**	*pen*
책 **chaek**	*book*	잡지 **japji**	*magazine*
가방 **gabang**	*bag*	소파 **sopa**	*sofa*
컴퓨터 **keompyuteo**	*computer*	전화 **jeonhwa**	*telephone*

13

Many words in modern Korean have been borrowed from English, for example "computer," "pen" and "sofa."

The pronunciation of these loan words has sometimes been slightly adapted to Korean speech patterns, but you can use or say the word as you would in English and be perfectly understood.

Language Focus

Korean nouns do not have articles *(a/an, the)*. Plurals are also simple. You can usually use the same word as the singular. So 책 **chaek** can mean *book, a book, the book, books,* or *the books*.

What does it mean?

Match the Korean with the pictures, then write the pronunciation and the English. as in the example.

가방 _____

컴퓨터 _____

문 _____

창문 *changmun   window(s)*

전화 _____

펜 _____

의자 _____

탁자 _____

소파 _____

텔레비전 _____

책 _____

잡지 _____

Word Square

Can you find the eight household words in the word square? Circle them and write the English, as in the example. The words can be horizontal or vertical.

리	에	파	소	젤	레	스	컴
엔	로	스	파	턴	싱	잡	지
욕	뉴	로	턴	버	다	캐	나
퓨	전	화	사	다	라	인	예
가	국	인	영	컴	퓨	터	인
방	마	자	의	스	버	캐	탁
전	헨	크	턴	버	다	의	자
텔	레	비	전	지	예	수	요

computer

_____

_____

_____

_____

_____

_____

Odd One Out

Which is the odd one out? Circle the word that doesn't belong in each row.

탁자 * 의자 * 소파 * 이름

한국 * 전화 * 호주 * 일본

사람 * 책 * 텔레비전 * 잡지

창문 * 수진 * 진희 * 사라

고맙습니다 * 천만에요 * 컴퓨터 * 안녕하세요

Language Focus

You have already met the question 뭐예요? **mwoyeyo?** (뭐 **mwo** *what* + 예요 **yeyo** *is*) in the expression 이름이 뭐예요? **ireumi mwoyeyo?** *what's your name?* To ask *what's this?* insert 이것이 **igeosi** *this (as for)* in place of the word 이름이 **ireum-i**.

> 이것이 뭐예요? **igeosi mwoyeyo?** *What's this?*

To answer, use the following:

이것은 **igeoseun** *this (as for)* + object + 이에요 **-ieyo** <u>or</u> 예요 **-yeyo**

If the word for the object ends with a consonant, for example 펜 **pen**, add 이에요 **-ieyo**. If it ends with a vowel, for example 소파 **sopa**, use 예요 **-yeyo**.

> 이것은 의자예요.
> **igeoseun uija-yeyo**
> *This is a chair./These are chairs.*
>
> 이것은 가방이에요.
> **igeoseun gabang-ieyo**
> *This is a bag./These are bags.*

To ask a question such as *Is this a chair?* just raise the intonation at the end of the sentence. Watch out for the Korean word 네 **ne** which means *"yes." "No"* is 아니오 **anio**. 이것이 **igeosi** can be shortened to 이게 **ige** in a question and 이것은 **igeoseun** is also often shortened to 이건 **igeon** or dropped altogether in the answer.

> 이게 문이에요? **ige mun-ieyo?** *Is this a door?*
> 네, 이건 문이에요. **ne, igeon mun-ieyo** *Yes, it's a door.*
> 아니오, 창문이에요. **anio, changmun-ieyo** *No, it's a window.*

Your turn to speak

Now ask what things are. Follow the prompts on your audio CD.

14

What is it?

Look at the photos of everyday objects from unusual angles. Then read the sentences and decide which picture they describe, as in the example.

1 이것은 의자예요. _e_

2 이것은 컴퓨터예요. _____

3 이것은 소파예요. _____

4 이것은 전화예요. _____

5 이건 문이에요. _____

6 이건 텔레비전이에요. _____

7 이건 펜이에요. _____

8 이건 가방이에요. _____

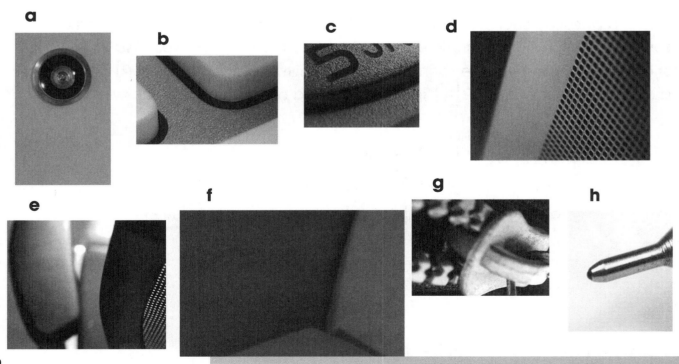

Key Words

15

녹차 **nokcha**	*green tea*	
커피 **keopi**	*coffee*	
샌드위치 **saendeuwichi**	*sandwich*	

케이크 **keikeu**	*cake*	
떡볶이 **tteokbokki**	*rice cake in spicy sauce*	
튀김 **twigim**	*deep-fried vegetables*	

 # Language Focus

To say *I'd like ...* use 주세요 **juseyo** (literally *"give"*) after the object you want.

커피 주세요. **keopi juseyo** *I'd like a coffee.*
녹차 주세요. **nokcha juseyo** *I'd like green tea.*

To ask for more than one item, link them using 과 **gwa** if the word before ends with a consonant, or 와 **wa** if it ends with a vowel.

튀김과 케이크 주세요.
twigim-gwa keikeu juseyo *I'd like twigim and a cake.*

커피와 녹차 주세요.
keopi-wa nokcha juseyo *I'd like a coffee and a green tea.*

The Korean equivalent of *Here you are* is 여기 있어요 **yeogi isseoyo** (**yeogi** = *here*; **isseoyo** = *is/have*).

떡볶이 주세요. **tteokbokki juseyo** *I'd like tteokbokki.*
여기 있어요. **yeogi isseoyo** *Here you are/Here it is.*
고맙습니다. **gomap-seumnida** *Thank you.*
천만에요. **cheonmaneyo** *You're welcome.*

Who orders what?

What are the customers ordering? Listen to your CD
and check what they order, as in the example.

16

	green tea	coffee	sandwich	cake	twigim (vegetables)	tteokbokki (rice cakes)
Customer 1	✓					✓
Customer 2						
Customer 3						
Customer 4						
Customer 5						

Now look at the table above and pretend you are ordering for yourself, for example:

녹차와 떡볶이 주세요. **nokcha-wa tteokbokki juseyo**

Unscramble the conversation

Can you put this conversation in the correct order?

a 안녕하세요. 커피 주세요.
annyeong-haseyo. keopi juseyo

b 고맙습니다.
gomap-seumnida

c 네, 이게 뭐예요?
ne, ige mwoyeyo?

d 커피와 튀김 여기 있어요.
keopi-wa twigim, yeogi isseoyo

e 커피요?
keopi-yo?

f 이건 튀김이에요.
igeon twigim-ieyo

g 안녕하세요.
annyeong-haseyo

h 튀김 주세요.
twigim juseyo

ORDER: _g,_ _____

Now check your answer with the conversation on your audio CD.

17

At the café

Your turn to order now. Look at the menu below and then you'll be ready to order from the waiter on your CD.

18

녹차

커피

샌드위치

케이크

떡볶이

튀김

The Café Game

1. Cut out the picture cards from Game Card 3.

2. Put the cards into a bag.

3. Shake the bag.

4. Pull out a card without looking.

5. Ask for the item on the card. For example:

녹차 주세요.

nokcha juseyo

I'd like a green tea.

6. If you can ask the question out loud quickly and fluently, then put the card aside. If not, then put it back into the bag.

7. See how long it takes you to get all of the cards out of the bag. You can also play with a friend and see who can collect the most cards.

GAME CARD **3** (see page 33)

Picture cards:

Key Words

방 **bang**	room	집 **jip**	house
냉장고 **naeng-jang-go**	refrigerator	나무 **namu**	tree
커튼 **keoteun**	curtains	차 **cha**	car
가스레인지 **gaseu-reinji**	cooker/hob	개 **gae**	dog
침대 **chimdae**	bed	쥐 **jwi**	mouse
그림 **geurim**	picture	고양이 **goyangi**	cat

19

Korean words can be a single syllable, such as 개 **gae** *(dog)* or 집 **jip** *(house)*. But more often they are a combination of two or more syllables. For example, 침대 **chimdae** *(bed)* consists of two syllables and 냉장고 **naeng-jang-go** *(refrigerator)* of three syllables.

The individual letters that make up a syllable are written together in a square shape. Look at page 90 for more details on how the individual letters are combined to form syllables.

Note that 차 **cha** can mean either *car* or *tea* (as in 녹차 **nokcha** *green tea*).

What does it mean?

Join the Korean to the pronunciation and write down the meaning in English.

커튼
차
개
침대
쥐
그림
집
방
냉장고
나무
가스레인지

jwi _____

chimdae _____

geurim _____

jip _____

keoteun *curtains*

gaseu-reinji _____

namu _____

naeng-jang-go _____

bang _____

cha _____

gae _____

What can you see?

Look at the picture and check (✔) the things you can see, as in the example.

침대 ☑   가방 ☐
의자 ☐   개 ☐
나무 ☐   냉장고 ☐
그림 ☐   고양이 ☐
탁자 ☐   방 ☐
소파 ☐   컴퓨터 ☐
커튼 ☐   펜 ☐
잡지 ☐   가스레인지 ☐
차 ☐   책 ☐

Read & **Speak**   **KOREAN**

Key Words

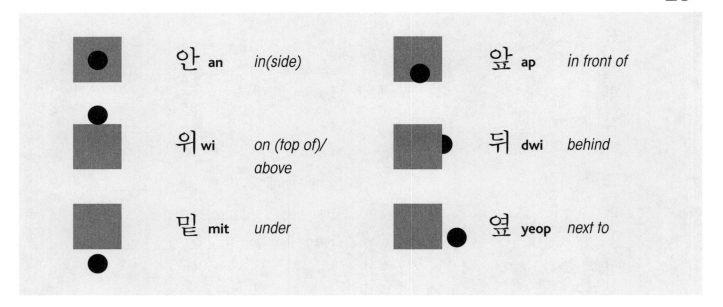

안 **an**   *in(side)*

위 **wi**   *on (top of)/ above*

밑 **mit**   *under*

앞 **ap**   *in front of*

뒤 **dwi**   *behind*

옆 **yeop**   *next to*

Language Focus

To say where something is in English we simply place the preposition (positional word) in the middle of the two objects: **The pen is _on the table_**. In Korean the preposition comes after the two objects and the order is **_"pen (as for) table on is."_** Notice as well that you need to use a small particle, 에 **-e**, after the preposition (**on, in,** etc.) to show that you are talking about a place.

> 펜은 의자 위에 있어요.
> **pen-eun uija wi-e isseoyo** *The pen is on the table.*
>
> 차는 집 앞에 있어요.
> **cha-neun jip ap-e isseoyo** *The car is in front of the house.*
>
> 개는 침대 밑에 있어요.
> **gae-neun chimdae mit-e isseoyo** *The dog is under the bed.*

Practice saying where things are on your CD.

Which word?

Put a circle around the word that correctly
describes each picture, as in the example.

차는 집 (앞에) 있어요.
뒤에

침대은 창문 위에 있어요.
밑에

그림은 소파 앞에 있어요.
위에

컴퓨터는 탁자 위에 있어요.
옆에

냉장고는 가스레인지 옆에 있어요.
위에

고양이는 의자 뒤에 있어요.
밑에

개는 차 안에 있어요.
위에

Language Focus

You have met a number of "subject particles" so far. These particles are placed directly after the subject of a sentence or question and roughly translate as **"as for."** They show what it is you are talking about. There are four subject particles – two used for words ending in vowels and two for words ending in consonants.

	subject particle	example
ends with vowel (e.g. 차 **cha** *car*)	가 **-ga**	차가 cha-ga
	는 **-neun**	차는 cha-neun
ends with consonant (e.g. 방 **bang** *room*)	이 **-i**	방이 bang-i
	은 **-eun**	방은 bang-eun

가 **-ga** and 이 **-i** are "neutral" subject particles whereas 는 **-neun** and 은 **-eun** are "emphatic." In the sentence 펜은 탁자 위에 있어요 **pen-eun takja wie isseoyo** *the pen is on the table*, 은 **-eun** emphasises the subject 펜 **pen**. If we change 은 **-eun** to the neutral 이 **-i**, the pen is no longer emphasized and the meaning is closer to the English ***there is a pen on the table***. Here are some examples. (Remember that to form questions simply raise the intonation at the end.)

차는 집 앞에 있어요. **cha-neun jip ape isseoyo**
The car is in front of the house.

차가 집 앞에 있어요. **cha-ga jip ape isseoyo**
There is a car in front of the house.

책은 침대 위에 있어요? **chaek -eun chimdae wie isseoyo**
Is the book on (top of) the bed?

책이 침대 위에 있어요? **chaek-i chimdae wie isseoyo**
Is there a book on (top of) the bed?

Look around the room you are in at the moment, or think of a room you know well. Can you describe where some of the things are, using the Korean sentences you have learned?

Where are the mice?

See how many mice you can find in the picture and make sentences about them as in the example.

Example:

쥐가 냉장고 앞에 있어요.

jwi-ga naeng-jang-go ape isseoyo

There's a mouse in front of the refrigerator.

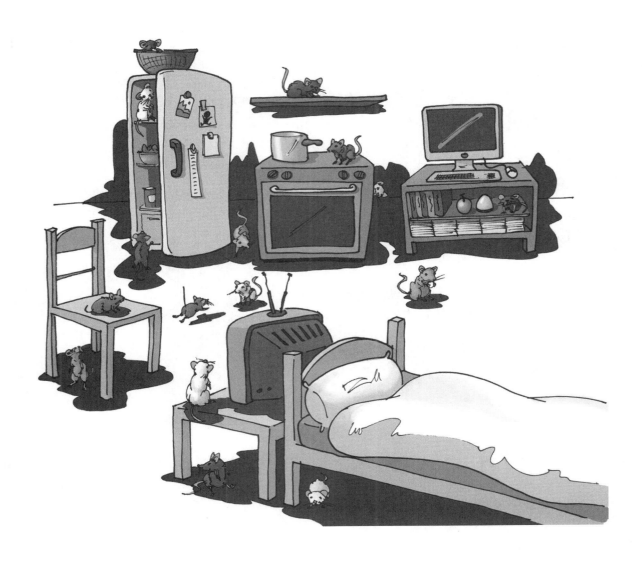

Language Focus

Generally, placing 안 **an** *(not)* before a verb will make it negative.

> 저는 한국에서 왔어요.
> **jeoneun hanguk-eseo wasseoyo**
> *I come from Korea. ("I-as for Korea-from came")*
>
> 저는 한국에서 안 왔어요.
> **jeoneun hanguk-eseo an wasseoyo**
> *I don't come from Korea. ("I-as for Korea-from not came")*

안 **an** combines with 이에요 **-ieyo** or 예요 **-yeyo** *(am/are/is)* to produce 아니에요 **anieyo**.

> 저는 미국사람이에요. **jeoneun miguk-saram-ieyo** *I'm American.*
> 저는 미국사람 아니에요. **jeoneun miguk-saram anieyo** *I'm not American.*
>
> 이것은/이건 소파예요. **igeoseun/igeon sopa-yeyo** *This is a sofa.*
> 이것은/이건 소파 아니에요. **igeoseun/igeon sopa anieyo** *This isn't a sofa.*

있어요 **isseoyo** *(there is/are ...)* has its own negative: 없어요 **eopsseoyo**.

> 차가 집 앞에 있어요. **chaga jip ape isseoyo**
> *There is a car in front of the house.*
>
> 차가 집 앞에 없어요. **chaga jip ape eopsseoyo**
> *There isn't a car in front of the house.*

No it isn't!

Practice disagreeing! Go to your audio CD and contradict all the statements you hear.

22

True or False?

Decide if the sentences describing the picture are true or false, as in the example.

	True	False
냉장고가 방 안에 있어요.	☑	☐
침대가 방 안에 있어요.	☐	☐
전화는 탁자 위에 있어요.	☐	☐
찬장이 없어요.	☐	☐
창문이 있어요.	☐	☐
쥐가 탁자 밑에 없어요.	☐	☐
나무가 집 뒤에 있어요.	☐	☐
가스 레인지는 냉장고 옆에 있어요.	☐	☐
개가 탁자 밑에 있어요.	☐	☐
텔레비전이 방에 없어요.	☐	☐

Language Review

You're half way through *Read & Speak Korean* – congratulations! This is a good time to summarize the main language points covered so far.

1 There is no clear distinction between plural and singular in Korean. 사람 **saram** means both *a person* and *people*.

2 It is important to include the subject particles: 가 **-ga** or 는 **-neun** for words ending with a vowel, and 이 **-i** or 은 **-eun** for those ending with a consonant. 은 **-eun** and 는 **-neun** are used to emphasize the subject.

3 The equivalent in Korean of *am/is/are* is the ending 예요 **-yeyo** (for words ending in a vowel) or 이에요 **-ieyo** (for words ending in a consonant). The opposite of both is 아니에요 **anieyo**. The equivalent of *there is/are* is 있어요 **isseoyo**. The opposite is 없어요 **eopsseoyo**.

> 저는 호주사람이에요.
> **jeoneun hoju-saram-ieyo** *I'm Australian.*
>
> 저는 호주사람 아니에요.
> **jeoneun hoju-saram anieyo** *I'm not Australian.*
>
> 쥐가 침대 밑에 있어요.
> **jwi-ga chimdae mit-e isseoyo** *There's a mouse under the bed.*
>
> 쥐가 침대 밑에 없어요.
> **jwi-ga chimdae mit-e eopsseoyo** *There isn't a mouse under the bed.*

4 In general you should use people's names rather than pronouns such as *he* or *she*. You don't generally need to use the pronoun *you* at all.

5 To ask questions, you simply raise the intonation at the end.

> 왕밍씨는 중국사람이에요?
> **wangmingssi-neun gungguk-saram-ieyo?**. *Is Wangming Chinese?*
>
> 영국 사람이에요? **yeongguk-saram-ieyo?** *Are (you) English?*

6 To request something, you can use the phrase 주세요 **juseyo** after the item(s) you want: 커피와 샌드위치 주세요. **keopi-wa saendeuwichi juseyo.** *I'd like a coffee and a sandwich.*

My Room

1. Tear out Game Card 4 at the back of your book and cut out the small pictures of items around the house (leave the sentence-build cards at the bottom of the sheet for the moment).

2. Stick the pictures wherever you like on the scene below.

3. Cut out the sentence-build cards from Game Card 4. Make as many sentences as you can describing your room. For example:

그림	이	침대	위에	있어요

geurim-i chimdae wie isseoyo
There's a picture above the bed.

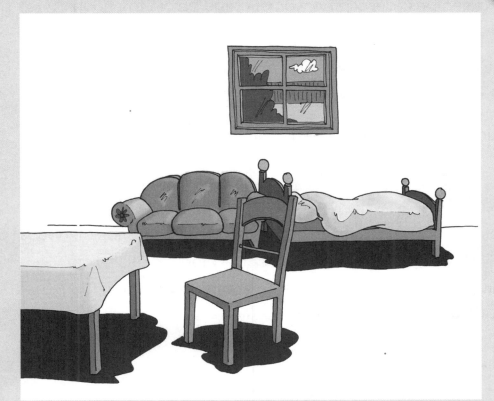

 ## Key Words

23

큰 **keun**	*big*		비싼 **bissan**	*expensive*		
작은 **jageun**	*small*		싼 **ssan**	*inexpensive*		
새 **sae**	*new*		아주 **aju**	*very*		
낡은 **nalgeun**	*old/worn out*		너무 **neomu**	*too*		

 ## Language Focus

As in English, Korean adjectives (descriptive words) come before the noun they describe.

> 큰 가방 **keun gabang** *big bag/big bags*
> 새 차 **sae cha** *new car/new cars*

아주 **aju** *(very)* is placed in front of the adjective, just like in English:

> 아주 싼 커피 **aju ssan keopi** *very inexpensive coffee*

Note that if an adjective is not used directly before the thing it describes, it needs a verb ending, usually 요 **-yo**. Adding **-yo** can affect the pronunciation. For example, 작은 **jageun** *(small)* changes to 작아요 **jagayo** *(to be small)*, 비싼 **bissan** *(expensive)* to 비싸요 **bissayo** *(to be expensive)*.

> 그건 비싸요. **geugeon bissayo** *That's expensive.*
> 그건 너무 작아요. **geugeon neomu jagayo** *That's too small.*

Can you remember?

Cover the Key Words panel on page 44. Then see if you can write out the pronunciation and meaning of the words below, as in the example.

비싼	b i s s a n	expensive
큰	k _ _ _	_____
낡은	n _ _ _ e _ _	_____
싼	_ s _ _	_____
새	_ _ e	_____
너무	n _ _ _ u	_____
아주	a _ _	_____
작은	_ _ g _ _ _	_____

What does it mean?

Match the Korean with the pictures. Then read the Korean out loud and write the English next to each, as in the example.

새 소파 _____

작은 커피 _____

작은 개 *(a) small dog* _____

낡은 차 _____

큰 나무 _____

작은 쥐 _____

큰 샌드위치 _____

비싼 그림 _____

\$500,000

Listen and check

Listen to the conversation at the car rental company and decide if these sentences are true or false.

A useful phrase you'll hear in the dialog is: 어때요? **eottaeyo?** *How is it?*. This is often used with the meaning of *How about...?*: 골프 어때요? *How about the Golf? ("The Golf, how is it?")*

		True	False
1	She thinks the Golf is too expensive.	☐	☐
2	She thinks the second car offered is too big.	☐	☐
3	She likes the Fiat.	☐	☐
4	The woman's name is Susie.	☐	☐
5	She's Canadian.	☐	☐

Unscramble the sentences

Look at the scrambled phrases from the conversation and write the correct order in the boxes. For example, *"How about the Golf"*:

b	a
어때요?	골프

1

☐	☐	☐
사람	이에요?	미국

2

☐	☐	☐
차	주세요	그

3

☐	☐	☐
저는	예요	메리

4

☐	☐	☐
작아요	그건	너무

Language Focus

You have already met the word 있어요 **isseoyo** with the meaning of *there is* or *there are.* You can also use this phrase to describe what you or other people have.

> 저는 낡은 탁자가 있어요.
> **jeoneun nalgeun takja-ga isseoyo** *I have an old table.*
>
> 수진씨는 새 컴퓨터가 있어요.
> **sujinssi-neun sae keompyuteo-ga isseoyo** *Sujin has a new computer.*
>
> 마이클씨는 비싼 차가 있어요.
> **maikeulssi-neun bissan chaga isseoyo** *Michael has an expensive car*

Remember that to ask a question, just raise the intonation at the end.

> 싼 차가 있어요?
> **ssan chaga isseoyo** *Do you have an inexpensive car?*
>
> 선영씨는 큰 집이 있어요?
> **seonyeongssi-neun keun jibi isseoyo** *Does Seonyeong have a big house?*

To give a short reply (*yes, I do*, etc.) you need to repeat 있어요 **isseoyo**.

> 새 차가 있어요?
> **sae chaga isseoyo** *Do you have a new car?*
>
> 네, 있어요.
> **ne, isseoyo** *Yes, (I) do.*

Now you can take part in a conversation with the car rental company. Follow the prompts on your audio CD.

25

 **Key Words**

26

머리 **meori**	*head/hair (on head)*	코 **ko**	*nose*
다리 **dari**	*legs*	입 **ip**	*mouth*
팔 **pal**	*arms*	귀 **gui**	*ears*
손가락 **son-garak**	*fingers*	배 **bae**	*stomach*
눈 **nun**	*eyes*	꼬리 **kkori**	*tail*

By now you're probably feeling much more confident about reading and speaking Korean. Maybe you'd like to try writing the letters and syllables for yourself. Although it's fun to copy the simpler shapes, you will need to get a guide to writing Korean in order to form the words correctly. The strokes should be completed in a certain order and will need practice to perfect.

Which word?

Circle the correct word to match the translation, as in the example.

1	*head/hair*	비싼	（머리）	커피	가방
2	*legs*	녹차	커튼	나무	다리
3	*stomach*	배	저	씨	펜
4	*mouth*	한	책	입	큰
5	*fingers*	냉장고	침대	작은	손가락
6	*tail*	는	새	집	꼬리
7	*ears*	문	귀	뭐	이
8	*nose*	코	최	국	개
9	*eyes*	긴	팀	박	눈
10	*arms*	방	차	팔	김

At the circus

Can you use the words in the box to complete the description of the clowns,
Cheolsu and Sunhi, as in the example?

1 배	**2** 커요
3 고양이	**4** 입
5 작아요	**6** 낡은

철수는 눈이 ___5___. _____ 가 커요.
그리고 손에 _____ 가방이 있어요.

순희는 코가 _____. _____ 이 작아요.
그리고 작은 _____ 가 있어요.

What does it look like?

What does the creature look like? Make as many sentences as you can describing the features it has.

We've included some more vocabulary you could use for your description.

Example:

아주 큰 코가 있어요.

aju keun koga isseoyo

(It) has a very big nose.

beautiful	아름다운	**areumdaun**
ugly	못생긴	**motsaenggin**
fat	뚱뚱한	**ttungttunghan**
thin	마른	**mareun**
long	긴	**gin**
short	짧은	**jjalbeun**
wings	날개	**nalgae**
feet	발	**bal**

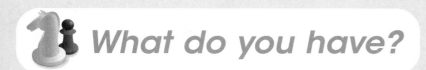

What do you have?

1 Cut out the picture cards from Game Card 5 and put them in a bag.

2 Cut out the adjective cards and put them in a different bag.

3 Pull out one card from each bag without looking.

4 Make a sentence to match the cards you have chosen, for example:

저는 낡은 컴퓨터가 있어요.
jeoneun nalgeun keompyuteo-ga isseoyo
I have an old computer.

5 Keep playing until all the cards have been chosen.

6 You can put the cards back in the bag and start again – each time the sentences will be different.

GAME CARD **5** (see page 53)

Picture cards:

Adjective cards:

큰	작은	새	낡은
비싼	싼	작은	아름다운
짧은	긴		

낡은

 ## Key Words

27

공항 **gonghang**	*airport*	공원 **gongwon**	*park*
학교 **hakgyo**	*school*	다리 **dari**	*bridge*
호텔 **hotel**	*hotel*	거리 **geori**	*street*
은행 **eunhaeng**	*bank*	버스 정거장 **beoseu jeong-geo-jang**	*bus stop*
박물관 **bakmulguan**	*museum*	근처 **geuncheo**	*nearby*
식당 **sikdang**	*restaurant*	...어디에 있어요? **... eodi-e isseoyo?**	*where's...?*
병원 **byeongwon**	*hospital*		
기차역 **gichayeok**	*train station*	저기에 **jeogi-e**	*over there*

You are new in town and are asking a Korean friend about the facilities. Follow the prompts on your audio CD.

28

window	computer
cupboard	table
chair	refrigerator
stove	sofa
bed	door
television	telephone

컴퓨터

kompyooto

창문

chang-moon

탁자

takja

찬장

chantjang

냉장고

neng-jang-gaw

의자

oo-ja

소파

sawpa

쿠커

koka

문

moon

침대

cheemdeh

전화기

chon-hwa-gee

텔레비전

tel-lebeejon

Language Focus

Notice the Korean word for *hotel*. This is an example of a 'loan' word borrowed from another language. Korean has borrowed many words, particularly from English. Look back at Topic 3. The words for *television, computer,* and *sandwich* are all examples of loan words.

You can recognize loan words when you hear Korean, although you need to bear in mind that the pronunciation of the words may be adapted to Korean speech patterns.

Questions and answers

Match the questions with their answers, as in the example.

은행이 어디에 있어요?   네, 식당 있어요.

근처에 식당 있어요?   공원은 학교 근처에 있어요.

근처에 호텔 있어요?   다리는 저기에 있어요.

공원이 어디에 있어요?   은행은 학교 옆에 있어요.

다리가 어디에 있어요?   네, 호텔은 기차역 앞에 있어요.

Key Words

택시 **taeksi**	taxi	비행기 **bihaeng-gi**	airplane
버스 **beoseu**	bus	배 **bae**	boat
기차 **gicha**	train	자전거 **jajeon-geo**	bicycle

Language Focus

Notice that the syllable 차 **cha** can be used by itself to mean *vehicle* or *car* and it can also be used in combination.

기차 **gicha**	train
마차 **macha**	horse-drawn carriage

The particle 로 **ro** is used after a mode of transportation to mean *by*.

차로 **cha-ro**	by car
택시로 **taeksi-ro**	by taxi
기차로 **gicha-ro**	by train

Word Square

Can you find the seven different means of transportation in the word square?
Write out the pronunciation and meaning for the words you have found, as in
the example.

은	에	처	소	항	버	스	요
어	자	전	거	턴	학	근	지
네	뉴	로	턴	에	다	캐	배
퓨	있	정	기	다	호	교	예
가	은	인	차	컴	퓨	비	인
택	시	자	의	에	버	행	탁
공	헨	크	기	리	다	기	자
처	버	비	전	차	예	텔	요

cha (car/vehicle)

_____

_____

_____

_____

_____

 Key Words

30

| 실례합니다 | excuse me! | 오른쪽으로 | on the right |
| sillye-hamnida | | oreunjjo-geuro | |

| ...에 어떻게 가요? | how do I get to...? | 왼쪽으로 | on the left |
| ...e eotteoke gayo? | | oenjjo-geuro | |

| ...가세요 | go... | 직진 하세요 | go straight ahead |
| ...gaseyo | | jikjin haseyo | |

| 첫 번째 골목 | the first street | 여기 yeogi | here |
| cheot beonjje golmok | | | |

| | | 그리고 geurigo | then |

| 두 번째 골목 | the second street | 그리고 나서 | after that |
| du beonjje golmok | | geurigo naseo | |

31

Ask for directions to places around town. Listen to the example and then follow the prompts on your audio CD.

Language Focus

In the phrase ...에 어떻게 가요? ...*e eotteoke gayo? (how do I get to...?)*,
에 **e** denotes the direction, 어떻게 **etteoke** means *how*, and 가요 **gayo** is the
verb *go* with the polite ending 요 **yo**. So the sentence reads ...*to how go?*

기차역에 어떻게 가요?
gichayeog-e eotteoke gayo? *How do I get to the train station?*

서울에 어떻게 가요?
seoul-e eotteoke gayo? *How do I get to Seoul?*

To answer the question, you can use the verb *go* again, this time with the ending
세요 **seyo**: 가세요 **gaseyo**. 세요 **seyo** is an "honorific" ending that you cannot use
when talking about yourself. You should use this polite ending when you are giving
someone directions or instructions.

왼쪽으로 가세요.
oenjjo-geuro gaseyo *Go/Turn left.* ("on the left go")

오른쪽으로 가세요.
oreunjjo-geuro gaseyo *Go/Turn right.* ("on the right go")

기차로 가세요.
gicha-ro gaseyo *Go by train.* ("train by go")

If you want to say *Take the first street on the right*, etc. you need to use the particle
에서 **eseo** *(at)* between *street* and *on the left/right.* Notice the slight change in
pronunciation (**golmok** + **eseo** = **golmo-geseo**).

첫 번째 골목에서 왼쪽으로 가세요.
cheot beonjje golmo-geseo oenjjo-geuro gaseyo
Take the first street on the left. ("first street at on the left go")

두 번째 골목에서 오른쪽으로 가세요.
du beonjje golmo-geseo oreunjjo-geuro gaseyo
Take the second street on the right.

Which way?

Make questions and answers, as in the example.

실례합니다. 기차역에 어떻게 가요?
sillye-hamnida. gicha-yeoge eotteoke gayo?
Excuse me, how do I get to the station?

 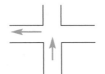

첫 번째 골목에서 왼쪽으로 가세요.
cheot beonjje golmo-geseo oenjjo-geuro gaseyo
Take the first street on the left.

1

2

 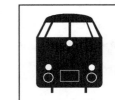

3

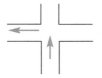 

4

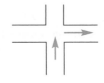

5

6

Around town

Below is a plan of a small town with some landmarks shown.
Starting from **You are here**, try to give directions to the following places:

기차역	병원	공원	버스 정거장
gicha-yeok*	**byeongwon**	**gongwon**	**beoseu jeong-geo-jang**
the station	*the hospital*	*the park*	*the bus stop*

(*The final **k** in **yeok** changes to **g** when endings are added – see pronunciation tips on page 91.)

For example, your directions to the station could be something like this:

직진하세요. 그리고 첫 번째 골목에서 오른쪽으로 가세요.
기차역은 다리 근처에 있어요.

jikjin haseyo. geurigo cheot beonjje golmo-geseo oreunjjo-geuro gaseyo.

gicha yeogeun dari geuncheo-e isseoyo.

Go straight ahead. Then take the first street on the right.

The station is near the bridge.

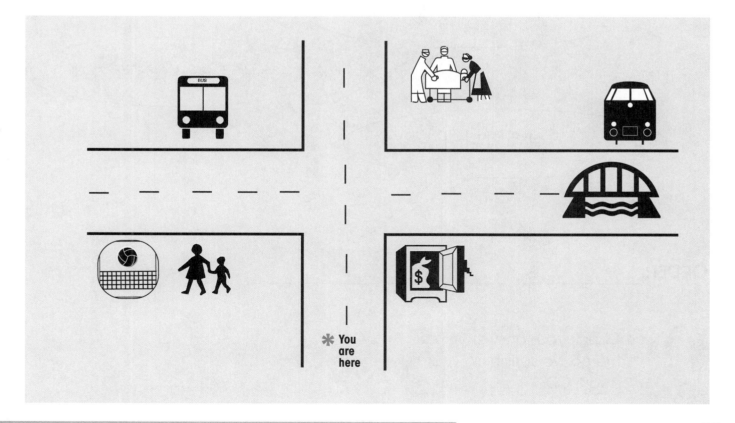

Unscramble the conversation

See if you can read the Korean in the word balloons. Then put the conversation in the correct order.

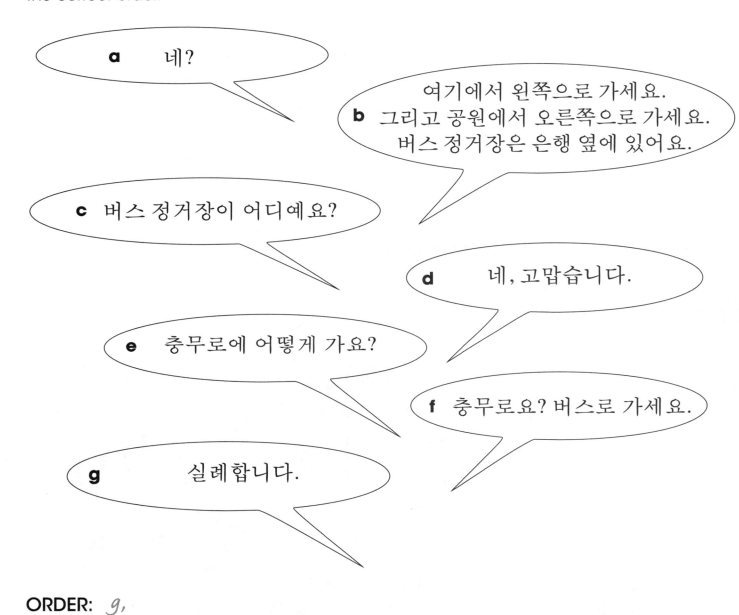

a 네?

b 여기에서 왼쪽으로 가세요.
그리고 공원에서 오른쪽으로 가세요.
버스 정거장은 은행 옆에 있어요.

c 버스 정거장이 어디예요?

d 네, 고맙습니다.

e 충무로에 어떻게 가요?

f 충무로요? 버스로 가세요.

g 실례합니다.

ORDER: _g,_ _____

Check your answer with the conversation on your audio CD.

32

33

Town Planning

1. Cut out the pictures of places around town from Game Card 6.

2. Listen to the first set of directions for the bank on your audio CD.

3. Pause the CD and stick the picture of the bank in the correct place on the town map on your game card.

4. Listen to the next set of directions and stick down the appropriate picture.

5. Repeat for all the directions until you have all your pictures stuck down on the map.

6. Looking at the completed map, you could try to give directions to the various places yourself. For example:

두 번째 골목에서 왼쪽으로 가세요.
은행은 학교 오른쪽 옆에 있어요.

du beonjjae golmo-geseo eonjjo-geuro gaseyo.
eunhaengeun hakgyo oreunjjok yeope isseoyo.
Take the second street on the left.
The bank is on the right, next to the school.

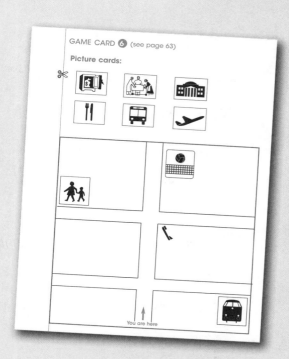

 **Key Words**

34

아내 anae	wife	여동생 yeo-dongsaeng	younger sister ("female younger sibling")
남편 nampyeon	husband	남동생 nam-dongsaeng	younger brother ("male younger sibling")
아이 ai	child		
딸 ttal	daughter	언니 eonni	older sister (for female)
아들 adeul	son	누나 nuna	older sister (for male)
어머니 eomeoni	mother	오빠 oppa	older brother (for female)
아버지 abeoji	father	형 hyeong	older brother (for male)

Korean has different words for "brother" and "sister" depending on whether they are older or younger. The words for older siblings also change depending on whether *you* are male or female. This means there are six words altogether: younger sister/younger brother/older brother (for female)/older sister (for female)/older brother (for male)/older sister (for male). See Key Words panel.

Language Focus

You can make sentences about your family using the verbs you've already met:
있어요 -isseoyo *is/has* and 없어요 eopsseoyo *isn't/hasn't* (see Topic 3).

> 저는 언니가 있어요. **jeoneun eonni-ga isseoyo**
> *I have an older sister/older sisters. (speaking as a female)*
>
> 저는 형이 없어요. **jeoneun hyeong-i eopsseoyo**
> *I don't have an older brother/older brothers. (speaking as a male)*
>
> 저는 아이가 없어요. **jeoneun ai-ga eopsseoyo**
> *I don't have any children.*

What does it mean?

Join the English to the pronunciation and the Korean script, as in the example.

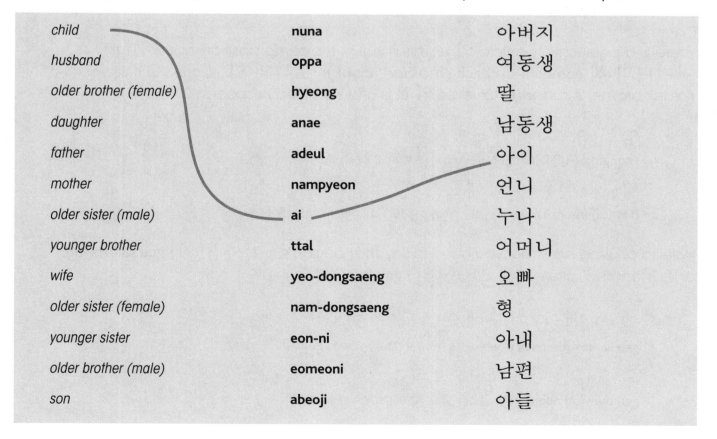

child	**nuna**	아버지
husband	**oppa**	여동생
older brother (female)	**hyeong**	딸
daughter	**anae**	남동생
father	**adeul**	아이
mother	**nampyeon**	언니
older sister (male)	**ai**	누나
younger brother	**ttal**	어머니
wife	**yeo-dongsaeng**	오빠
older sister (female)	**nam-dongsaeng**	형
younger sister	**eon-ni**	아내
older brother (male)	**eomeoni**	남편
son	**abeoji**	아들

Language Focus

Remember that Koreans generally avoid using the subject *you* when speaking. Instead they normally use a title (e.g., 씨 **si** *Mr./Mrs./Miss*) after the name or omit it altogether. In the same way, there's no need to include an equivalent of *your*.

> 집이 어디예요?
> **jibi eodi-yeyo?** *Where is (your) house?*

> 마이클 브라운 씨, 남동생이에요?
> **maikeul beurawun-ssi, nam-dongsaeng-ieyo?**
> *Mr. Michael Brown, is it (your) younger brother?*

Use 제 **je** *(my)* to say something *belongs to me.*

> 이건 제 컴퓨터예요. **igeon je keompyuteo-yeyo**
> *This is my computer.* ("this my computer it is")

> 제 어머니예요. **je eomeoni-yeyo**
> *It's my mother.* ("my mother it is")

There is a possessive particle 의 **ui**. This is put in the same position as the English *'s*: 어머니의 책 **eomeoni-ui chaek** *(mother's book)*; 오빠의 학교 **oppa-ui hakgyo** *(older brother's school)*. However, 의 **ui** is often omitted in speech.

> 영민(의) 자전거예요.
> **yeongmin(-ui) jajeongeo-yeyo** *It's Yeongmin's bicycle.*

> 딸(의) 이름이 뭐예요?
> **ttal-(ui) ireum-i mwo-yeyo?** *What's (your) daughter's name?*

Instead of using *his* or *her* you need to say *that person's*: 그 사람(의) **geu saram(-ui)**, or its "honorific" alternative: 그 분(의) **geu bun(-ui)**.

> 그 사람(의) 친구예요.
> **geu saram-(ui) chingu-yeyo** *It's his/her (that person's) friend.*

> 그 분(의) 아들예요.
> **geu bun-(ui) adeul-yeyo** *It's his/her (that person's) son.*

Family Tree

Make up sentences about this family, as in the example.

이 진희씨는 김 민수씨(의) 아내예요.
i jinhisi-neun gim minsu-ssi(-ui) anae-yeyo
Jinhi Lee is Minsu Gim's wife.

김 민수   이 진희

영철   수진

Robert's family

Listen to Robert answering questions about his family.
Circle the correct names on the family tree, as in the example.

35

팀
마크
로버트

리사
사라
헨렌

켄
진희
(로버트)

영철
마크
진희

Questions and answers

Now read the questions on the left and then match them to the answers on the right that Robert gave, as in the example.

형 있어요?	제 어머니 이름은 사라예요.
어머니 이름이 뭐예요?	아니오, 누나 없어요.
누나 있어요?	아버지 이름은 팀이에요.
형 이름이 뭐예요?	저는 미국 시카고에서 왔어요.
아버지 이름이 뭐예요?	저는 로버트예요.
이름이 뭐예요?	형 이름은 마크예요.
어디에서 왔어요?	네, 있어요.

Language Focus

To ask someone politely *who's this?* use the phrase 이 분은 누구세요? **i bun-eun nuguseyo?** 이 분 **i bun** is the honorific way of saying *this person* (see page 66 for *that person*) and 누구세요? **nuguseyo** is a combination of 누구? **nugu** *(who?)* and the honorific ending 세요 **seyo**.

이 분은 누구세요? **i bun-eun nuguseyo?** *Who's this?*

제 누나예요. **je nuna-yeyo** *It's my sister.*

제 친구, 신 민선씨예요.
je chingu, sin minseon-ssi-yeyo *It's my friend, Mrs./Miss Minseon Sin.*

When introducing a sibling, you don't need to use the title with the name. But if introducing a senior member of the family, such as parents or grandparents, Koreans wouldn't normally give names at all, but instead use the honorific ending 세요 **seyo**, for example 제 아버지세요 **je abeoji-seyo** *It's my father.*

Look at the this conversation. (Note also how to say *pleased to meet you*.)

— 안녕하세요, 상준씨?
annyeong-haseyo, sangjun-ssi *Hello, Sangjun.*

— 안녕하세요, 제인씨. 이 분은 누구세요?
annyeong-haseyo, jein-ssi. i bun-eun nuguseyo? *Hello, Jane. Who's this?*

— 제 남동생 마크예요.
je nam-dongsaeng makeu-yeyo *This is my younger brother, Mark*

— 만나서 반갑습니다, 마크씨.
mannaseo bangap-seumnida, makeu-ssi *Pleased to meet you, Mark.*

— 만나서 반갑습니다, 상준씨.
mannaseo bangap-seumnida, sangjun-ssi *Pleased to meet you, Sangjun.*

Now introduce <u>your</u> family using the conversation above as a guide. Follow the prompts on your audio CD.

36

 **Key Words**

하나 hana	one	일곱 ilgop	seven
둘 dul	two	여덟 yeodeol	eight
셋 set	three	아홉 ahop	nine
넷 net	four	열 yeol	ten
다섯 daseot	five	열하나 yeol-hana	eleven
여섯 yeoseot	six	열둘 yeol-dul	twelve

 Language Focus

There are two sets of numbers in Korean. Above are the "pure" Korean ones. An alternative "Sino" set of numbers exists borrowed from the Chinese language (e.g., one = 일 **il**, two = 이 **i**). However, as a beginner you can start with the Korean set.

If you are using the numbers in the abstract, they can be used as above. But if you want to count things or people, you have to include a "classifier." Classifiers are put after the number and are similar to words in English such *as a <u>bar</u> (of chocolate), a <u>roll</u> (of film)*. The most common classifier is 개 **gae** *(thing)*, but when you count people you need to use either 명 **myeong** (plain) or 분 **bun** (honorific).

> 아이 다섯 명 **ai daseot-myeong** *five children.*
> 펜 열여섯 개 **pen yeol-yeoseot gae** *16 ("ten-six") pens*

The spelling of the numbers one to four changes slightly when a classifier is used:
하나 **hana** ➔ 한 **han**; 둘 **dul** ➔ 두 **du**; 셋 **set** ➔ 세 **se**; 넷 **net** ➔ 네 **ne**.

> 저는 펜이 두 개 있어요. **jeoneun pen-i du gae isseoyo** *I have two pens.*
> 저는 언니가 세 명 있어요. **jeoneun eonni-ga se myeong isseoyo**
> *I have three older sisters.*

How many?

Match the numbers with the pronunciation, as in the example.

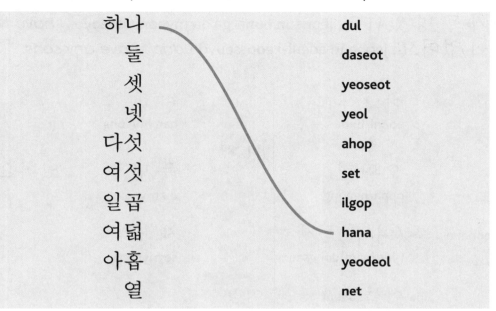

하나	dul
둘	daseot
셋	yeoseot
넷	yeol
다섯	ahop
여섯	set
일곱	ilgop
여덟	hana
아홉	yeodeol
열	net

Korean sums

Circle the correct answer to these sums, as in the example.

1 하나 **+** 넷 **=** 하나 둘 셋 넷 (다섯) 여섯 일곱 여덟 아홉 열 열하나 열둘

2 둘 **+** 여섯 **=** 하나 둘 셋 넷 다섯 여섯 일곱 여덟 아홉 열 열하나 열둘

3 셋 **X** 둘 **=** 하나 둘 셋 넷 다섯 여섯 일곱 여덟 아홉 열 열하나 열둘

4 아홉 **+** 셋 **=** 하나 둘 셋 넷 다섯 여섯 일곱 여덟 아홉 열 열하나 열둘

5 열둘 **-** 열 **=** 하나 둘 셋 넷 다섯 여섯 일곱 여덟 아홉 열 열하나 열둘

6 여덟 **+** 둘 **=** 하나 둘 셋 넷 다섯 여섯 일곱 여덟 아홉 열 열하나 열둘

7 다섯 **-** 셋 **=** 하나 둘 셋 넷 다섯 여섯 일곱 여덟 아홉 열 열하나 열둘

8 열하나 **-** 열 **=** 하나 둘 셋 넷 다섯 여섯 일곱 여덟 아홉 열 열하나 열둘

9 셋 **X** 셋 **=** 하나 둘 셋 넷 다섯 여섯 일곱 여덟 아홉 열 열하나 열둘

My family

Use the table below to make sentences about yourself, as in the examples.

저는 누나가 두 명 있어요. **jeoneun nuna-ga du myeong isseoyo** *I have two sisters.*

저는 아들이 없어요. **jeoneun adeul-i eopsseoyo** *I don't have any sons.*

저는 jeoneun	언니/누나 eonni/nuna		한 명 han myeong	
		가 -ga		
	오빠/형 oppa/hyeong		두 명 du myeong	있어요 isseoyo
	(여/남)동생 (yeo/nam)dongsaeng		세 명 se myeong	
	아들 adeul	이 -i		
	딸 ttal			
	아이 ai			없어요 eopsseoyo

Listen and speak

Now imagine you are with some of your family looking for the station and you meet a Korean friend.

38

Carefully prepare the information below that you will need to take part in the conversation. Then go to your audio CD and see how you get on introducing your family.

1 Think of two members of your family – one male and one female. For example, your husband and your daughter; or your brother and your mother.

2 How would you tell someone their names in Korean?

3 How would you ask *how do I get to the station*?

4 How do you say *thank you* and *goodbye*?

You can repeat the conversation, but this time use two different members of your family and ask how to get to the bus stop.

Bingo!

1. Cut out the small number tokens and the bingo cards on Game Card 7.

2. Find 16 buttons for each player or make 16 small blank pieces of card (to cover the squares on the bingo card).

3. Put the tokens into a bag and shake thoroughly.

4. Pull out a number token and say the number out loud in Korean.

5. If you have that number on your card, cover the square with a button or blank piece of card. If you have more than one square with that number, you can only cover one.

6. Put the number token back in the bag and shake again.

7. Repeat steps 3–6 until you have all the squares covered on the bingo card. Then you can shout:
이겼다! **igyeotta!** *I've won!*

You can play with a friend or challenge yourself.

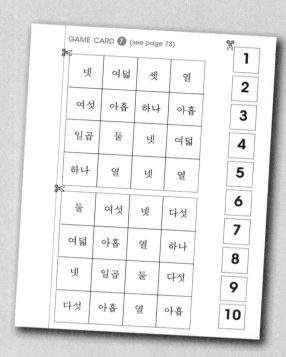

Key Words

39

교사 **gyo-sa**	teacher	운전사 **unjeon-sa**	driver
학생 **haksaeng**	student	회사원 **hoesawon**	office worker
의사 **ui-sa**	doctor	점원 **jeomwon**	store assistant
요리사 **yori-sa**	chef	엔지니어 **enjinieo**	engineer
회계사 **hoegye-sa**	accountant	배우 **bae-u**	actor

If your occupation or those of your family aren't listed here, try to find out what they are in Korean.

What does it mean?

Join the Korean to the pronunciation and the English, as in the example.

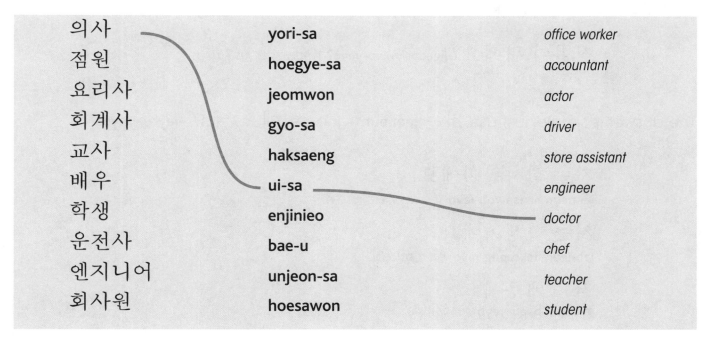

의사	yori-sa	office worker
점원	hoegye-sa	accountant
요리사	jeomwon	actor
회계사	gyo-sa	driver
교사	haksaeng	store assistant
배우	ui-sa	engineer
학생	enjinieo	doctor
운전사	bae-u	chef
엔지니어	unjeon-sa	teacher
회사원	hoesawon	student

The tools of the trade

Match the jobs to the tools of the trade, as in the example.

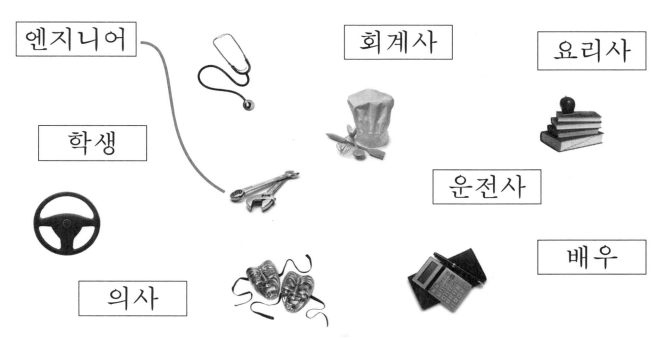

엔지니어

회계사

요리사

학생

운전사

의사

배우

Language Focus

The Korean for *job* is easy to remember: 직업 **jigeop**. To make a question, just add 뭐예요? **mwo-yeyo?** *(what?)*.

> 직업이 뭐예요? **jigeop-i mwo-yeyo?** *What's your job?*

The answer is simple: just use 저는 **jeoneun** + job +이에요/예요 **-ieyo/-yeyo**.

저는 회사원이에요.
jeoneun hoesawon-ieyo *I'm an office worker.*

저는 학생이에요.
jeoneun haksaeng-ieyo *I'm a student.*

저는 배우예요.
jeoneun baeu-yeyo *I'm an actor.*

Other possible answers include:

퇴직 했어요.
toejik haesseoyo *I'm retired.*

직업이 없어요.
jigeobi eopsseoyo *I don't have a job at the moment.*

집에서 일해요.
jibeseo il-haeyo *I work from home.*

40

Listen and note

Listen to two people telling you about themselves
and fill out the details in English on the forms below.

First Name: ...*Chanho*.........................

Family name: ....

Nationality: ....

Name of spouse: ....

No. of children: ....

Occupation: ....

First Name: ....

Family name: ....

Nationality: ....

Name of spouse: ....

No. of children: ....

Occupation: ....

Your turn to speak

41

Now you give same information about yourself.
Follow the prompts on your audio CD.

What's the answer?

Match the questions to the answers.

For example: **1d**

1 이름이 뭐예요?

2 어디에서 왔어요?

3 아내 이름이 뭐예요?

4 아이가 있어요?

5 직업이 뭐예요?

a 네, 아들이 한 명, 딸이 두 명 있어요.

b 저는 배우예요.

c 제 아내 이름은 저스틴이에요.

d 제 이름은 헤리예요.

e 저는 호주에서 왔어요.

Which word?

Write the correct number of the word in the box to complete the description, as in the example.

1 아내	**2** 아들	**3** 이름
4 아이	**5** 두 명	**6** 배우

제 __3__ 은 헤리예요. 저는 _____ 입니다. 저는 호주 멜본에서 왔어요. 제 _____ 이름은 저스틴이에요. 그리고 저는 _____ 가 세 명 있어요. _____ 한 명, 딸 _____ 있어요.

 **Key Words**

공장 **gongjang**	factory	대학교 **daehakgyo**	college
가게 **gage**	store	회사 **hoesa**	company
극장 **geukjang**	theater		
사무실 **samusil**	office		

Look back as well at the Key Words on page 54 for other places of work.

 Language Focus

To say where you work use the particle 에서 **eseo** *(at)* with the verb 일해요 **il-haeyo**, meaning *work*.

> 저는 의사예요. 병원에서 일해요.
> **jeoneun uisa-yeyo. byeongwon-eseo il-haeyo**
> *I'm a doctor. I work in a hospital.*

To say where the place of work is, you need to add 에 있는 **e in-neun** after the name of the town or country: *town/country* + **e in-neun** + *place of work* + **eseo** + **il-haeyo**.

> 부산에 있는 큰 회사에서 일해요.
> **busan-e in-neun keun hoesa-eseo il-haeyo**
> *I work for a large company in Busan.*

To ask where someone else works use 어디? **eodi** *(where?)* with 일해요 **il-haeyo**, or its honorific form 일하세요 **il-haseyo** to show more deference.

> 어디에서 일해요/일하세요?
> **eodi-eseo il-haeyo/il-haseyo?** *Where do you work? ("where at work?")*

Word Square

Can you find the 8 different work places in the word square?
Words can read horizontally or vertically.
Write out the meaning for the words you have found.

병	명	처	공	장	버	니	학
원	입	틴	거	턴	있	근	교
은	뉴	가	턴	식	당	캐	요
사	무	실	는	다	는	교	멜
멜	입	인	차	주	입	극	인
택	가	자	주	에	버	장	탁
공	게	크	교	리	다	기	자
주	제	비	교	은	행	제	요

factory _____

_____

_____

_____

_____

_____

_____

_____

Now make sentences for each of the work places, as in the example:

저는 엔지니어예요. 공장에서 일 해요.
jeoneun enjinieo-yeyo. gongjang-eseo il haeyo.
I'm an engineer. I work in a factory.

What are they saying?

Match the people with what they are saying. For example: **1e**

1 저는 인천에 있는 레스토랑에서 일 해요.

2 저는 영국에 있는 학교에서 일 해요.

3 저는 아일랜드에 있는 극장에서 일 해요.

4 저는 캐나다에 있는 공장에서 일 해요.

5 저는 미국 은행에서 일 해요.

6 저는 부산에 있는 가게에서 일 해요.

a

b

c

d

e

f

Listen and speak

43

Imagine you are a chef. You're meeting someone for the first time and they are asking you about yourself.

Carefully prepare the information below that you will need to take part in the conversation. Then go to your audio CD and see how you get on talking about yourself.

1 Your name is Byeongsu Kim (김 병수).

2 You're from Busan.

3 You're a chef.

4 You work in a Korean restaurant in New York.

5 You have two daughters.

6 Your wife is a teacher in a big school.

Which word?

Now write the correct number of the word in the box to complete the description of Byeongsu's life, as in the example.

1 대학교	**2** 요리사	**3** 학교에서	**4** 아내
5 예요	**6** 일 해요	**7** 딸	**8** 근처

제 이름은 김 병수 __5__. 저는 _____예요. 한국 부산에서 왔어요.

저는 뉴욕에 있는 한국 식당에서 _____ 제 _____ 는 선생님이에요.

식당 _____ 에 있는 아주 큰 _____ 일 해요.

저희는 _____ 이 두 명 있어요. 둘 다 _____ 학생이에요.

Where do I work?

1. Tear out the work-place picture cards and profession word cards on Game Card 8.

2. Turn the cards face down on a table, with the pictures on one end of the table and the words on the other.

3. Turn a word card and make a sentence with the profession as appropriate, e.g. 저는 교사예요. *jeoneun gyosa-yeyo* (*I'm a teacher*).

4. Then turn over a picture card. If the work-place picture matches the profession, say 저는 ...에서 일 해요. *jeoneun ...-eseo il haeyo* (*I work in a/an ...*), e.g. 저는 학교에서 일 해요. *jeoneun hakgyo-eseo il haeyo* (*I work in a school*).

5. If you turn over a matching picture and say both sentences correctly, you get to keep the cards. If you don't, you must turn the cards face down and try again.

6. The winner is the one who collects the most cards.

7. You can compete with a friend or challenge yourself against the clock.

(Review the vocabulary on pages 54, 56 and 74 before you play the game.)

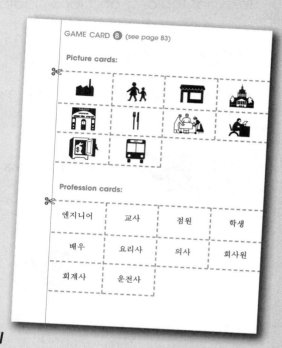

GAME CARD **8** (see page 83)

Picture cards:

Profession cards:

엔지니어	교사	점원	학생
배우	요리사	의사	회사원
회계사	운전사		

학교

This *Test Yourself* section reviews all the Korean you have learned in this program. Have a go at the activities. If you find you have forgotten something, go back to the relevant topic(s) and look again at the **Key Words** and **Language Focus** panels.

May I have...?

Ask for the following, as in the example:

차 주세요. **cha juseyo**

1

2 green

3

4

5

6

44

Listen and check

Listen to Jinhi talking about herself and decide if the following sentences are true or false.

		True	False
1	Jinhi is Korean.	☐	☐
2	She comes from a small town.	☐	☐
3	She's a teacher.	☐	☐
4	She works in France.	☐	☐
5	Her husband is an engineer.	☐	☐
6	She has five children.	☐	☐

Which word?

Now write the correct number of the word in the box to complete the description of Jinhi, as in the example.

1 큰	**2** 남편	**3** 한 명	**4** 병원
5 아이	**6** 딸	**7** 한국	**8** 교사

저는 박 진희예요. _7_ 에 있는 ＿＿ 도시 인천에서 왔어요.

저는 ＿＿ 예요. 영국에 있는 작은 한국학교에서 일 해요.

제 ＿＿ 은 의사예요. 한국학교 옆에 있는 큰 ＿＿ 에서 일 해요.

저희는 ＿＿ 가 네 명 있어요. 아들 ＿＿ 그리고 ＿＿ 이 세 명이에요.

Can you try and make up a similar description about yourself?

Read and check

Look at the picture and decide if the sentences are true or false.
Look back at topics 4–6 if you are unsure of any of the words.

	True	False
1 그림에 은행이 있어요.	☐	☐
2 병원이 은행의 오른쪽 옆에 있어요.	☐	☐
3 학교가 은행의 왼쪽 옆에 있어요.	☐	☐
4 골목에 개가 있어요.	☐	☐
5 골목에 차가 없어요.	☐	☐
6 차 위에 작은 고양이가 있어요.	☐	☐
7 학교 뒤에 큰 나무가 있어요.	☐	☐
8 병원 앞에 낡은 자전거가 있어요.	☐	☐

What does it mean?

Can you remember these words? Join the words and write the pronunciation next to the Korean, as in the example

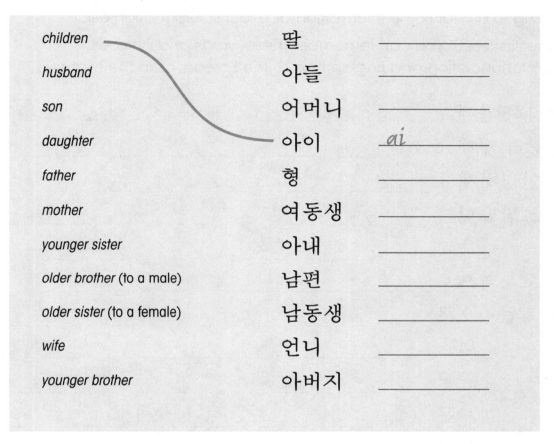

children	딸	_____
husband	아들	_____
son	어머니	_____
daughter	아이	*ai*
father	형	_____
mother	여동생	_____
younger sister	아내	_____
older brother (to a male)	남편	_____
older sister (to a female)	남동생	_____
wife	언니	_____
younger brother	아버지	_____

How do you say it?

Now see if you can say these in Korean, as in the example.

1 My husband is a doctor.
제 남편은 의사예요.
je nampyeon-eun uisa-yeyo

2 I have a younger sister.

3 My son is an engineer.

4 Jinhi's mother is from Daejeon.

5 My wife's name is Claire.

6 My older brother is an actor.

7 I don't have any children.

8 I have three daughters.

At the tourist information office

45

Finally, you are going to test your new Korean conversational skills by joining in the dialog on your audio CD.

You're going to ask for some information at a tourist information office.

To prepare, first see if you can remember these words and phrases.
Write the pronunciation and English next to the Korean, as in the example.

Korean	Pronunciation and English
안녕히 가세요	*annyeong-hi gaseyo goodbye (to s.o. leaving)*
안녕히 계세요	
안녕하세요	
고맙습니다	
뒤	
오른쪽으로	
왼쪽으로	
버스	
근처	
큰	
박물관	
어디?	

Now follow the prompts on your audio CD. Don't worry if you don't manage everything the first time around. Just keep repeating it until you are fluent.

Congratulations on successfully completing this introductory **Read & Speak Korean** program. You have overcome the obstacle of learning an unfamiliar language and a different script. You should now have the confidence to enjoy using the Korean you have learned. You have also acquired a sound basis from which to expand your language skills in whichever direction you choose. Good luck!

This **Reference** section gives an overview of the Korean script and pronunciation. You can use it to refer to as you work your way through the **Read & Speak Korean** program. Don't expect to take it all in from the beginning. **Read & Speak Korean** is designed to build your confidence step by step as you progress through the topics. The details will start to fall into place gradually as you become more familiar with the Korean script and language.

The Korean script

The Korean script, more properly called the *Hangeul* script, is not nearly as difficult as it might seem at first glance. Although Korean used to be written in Chinese characters (*Hanja*), these are now only rarely used and everyday material is written in the Hangeul alphabet developed in the 15th century.

The main difference between the way Hangeul is written and most other scripts, is that each syllable of a word is written together to form a square shape – the written shape most familiar to most 15th-century Koreans.

The alphabet: consonants

There are 14 consonants (non-vowels) in the Hangeul alphabet, plus five double letters.

Here are the consonants with their pronunciation. Where a letter has two pronunciations shown, these alternatives are used at the beginning or end of a syllable – see page 91 for more detail.

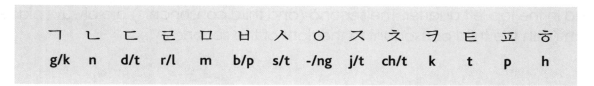

ㄱ	ㄴ	ㄷ	ㄹ	ㅁ	ㅂ	ㅅ	ㅇ	ㅈ	ㅊ	ㅋ	ㅌ	ㅍ	ㅎ
g/k	n	d/t	r/l	m	b/p	s/t	-/ng	j/t	ch/t	k	t	p	h

Here are the five double consonants.

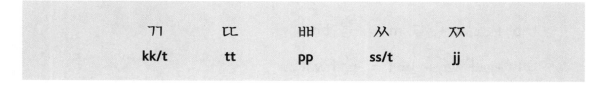

ㄲ	ㄸ	ㅃ	ㅆ	ㅉ
kk/t	tt	pp	ss/t	jj

The alphabet: vowels and diphthongs

There are ten vowels in the Hangeul alphabet, plus a number of diphthongs (vowel combinations). Here are ten main vowels with their pronunciation.

ㅏ	ㅑ	ㅓ	ㅕ	ㅗ	ㅛ	ㅜ	ㅠ	ㅡ	ㅣ
a	ya	eo	yeo	o	yo	u	yu	eu	i

Here are the diphthongs. You will quickly start to recognize the most common.

ㅐ	ㅔ	ㅒ	ㅖ	ㅘ	ㅝ	ㅙ	ㅚ	ㅞ	ㅟ	ㅢ
ae	e	yae	ye	wa	wo	wae	oe	we	wi	ui

Syllables

Korean words are made up of one or more syllables. The syllables are composed of the letters written in a square shape according to certain rules. It is useful to be familiar with these rules, but don't worry about trying to memorize them at this point.

A syllable has to start with a consonant (which can be the silent consonant ㅇ – see pronunciation). There are two, or occasionally three, consonants, but only one vowel (diphthongs included).

If the vowel is written with a vertical line, it is placed to the right of the consonant; if with a horizontal line, it is placed under the consonant. If both lines appear, the consonant is placed in the top left quarter. The second (and third consonants) are always placed at the bottom (with the third consonant to the right of the second),

ㄴ n + ㅏ a = 나 na

ㅅ s + ㅟ wi = 쉬 swi

ㅂ b + ㅗ o + ㅁ m = 봄 bom

ㅎ h + ㅘ wa + ㄹ l = 활 hwal

ㅇ – + ㅏ a + ㄴ n + ㅈ j = 앉 an(j)

Pronunciation

Some elements of Korean pronunciation need special attention.

The consonants shown with two alternative pronunciations on page 89 (except **r/l**) are pronounced as the first alternative when they are the initial consonant in a syllable, and as the second alternative for a final consonant.

가요 **gayo** *go*   국 **guk** *soup*

일본 **ilbon** *Japan*   밥 **bap** *rice/food*

When ㄹ **r/l** is surrounded by vowels "**r**" is pronounced. Otherwise, "**l**" is pronounced.

나라 **nara** *country*   서울 **seoul** *Seoul*

ㅅ **s** is pronounced "**sh**" when followed by the vowels ㅑ , ㅕ , ㅛ, ㅠ, or ㅣ .

신 **shin** *Shin (surname)*   쇼 **shyo** *show*

Note also that the final consonants **t** and **k** are not pronounced strongly and that double consonants (see page 89) sound much tighter than the single equivalents.

When the letter ㅇ is the first consonant it is silent. Only the vowel sound is pronounced. When the second consonant, it is pronounced **ng** as in *song*.

아버지 **abeoji** *father*   은행 **eunhaeng** *bank*

The three letters ㄱ, ㄷ, and ㅂ are half aspirated and half voiced, and sound somewhere between **g, d, b** and **k, t, p**.

Some Korean vowels sound very similar. ㅔ **e** and ㅐ **ae** are both pronounced **ae** as in *bare*; ㅖ **ye** and ㅒ **yae** are both pronounced **yae** as in *yeah*; ㅞ **we**, ㅙ **wae** and ㅚ **oe** are all pronounced **wae** as in *where*.

When certain syllables combine in a word, there can be changes to the pronunciation. This is known as "linking." Two important changes are:

- When the consonant ㅂ **b/p** is followed by the consonant ㄴ **n**, the ㅂ is pronounced **m**. For example, in the word for *thank you*: 고맙습니다 **gomap-seumnida** (not **gomap-seupnida**).

- When a syllable within a word begins with the silent ㅇ , the final consonant of the previous syllable replaces the silent ㅇ . If this is one of the consonants with alternative initial and final pronunciations (see above), it will be pronounced with its *initial* sound. For example, 이것 **igeot** *(this)* + 이 **i** *(as for)* = 이것이 **igeosi**.

You will find an introduction to the sounds of Korean on track 1 of your audio.

1

ANSWERS

Topic 1

Page 6
Check your answers with the Key Words panel on page 5.

Page 8: What are they saying?

Page 8: What do you hear?
You should have checked boxes 1 and 3.

Page 10: What does it mean?
1b, 2c 3e, 4f, 5a 6d

Page 10: Which word?

안녕 ___2___.

___5___ 하세요.

___4___최 진만이에요. 이름이 ___3___?

김수정 ___1___.

Page 11: What are their names?
사라	**sara** Sarah	팀	**tim** Tim
헨렌	**hellen** Helen	켄	**ken** Ken
메리	**meri** Mary	마크	**makeu** Mark
리사	**lisa** Lisa	로버트	**robeoteu** Robert

Page 12: In or out?
IN: Sarah, Sujin, Tim, Minjun, Yeongcheol
OUT: Raj, Michael, Helen, Robert, Jinhi

Topic 2

Page 15: Where are the countries?
캐나다 _1_   아일랜드 _3_   영국 _4_   중국 _5_

일본 _6_   한국 _7_   호주 _8_   미국 _2_

Page 16: How do you say it?
Check your answers with the Key Words panel on page 14.

Page 16: Which city?
런던	London
부산	Busan
시드니	Sydney
워싱턴	Washington
서울	Seoul
로스 엔젤레스	Los Angeles
뉴욕	New York

Page 17: Audio track 8
Jinhi Park: Korea; Michael: America; Kyoko: Japan;
Jane: England; Wangming: China; Ken: Canada

Page 18: Where are they from?

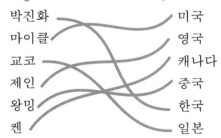

Page 20: Who's from where?

1 피터씨는 미국 뉴욕에서 왔어요.
   piteossi-neun miguk nyuyok-eseo wasseoyo

2 교코씨는 일본 오사카에서 왔어요.
   gyokossi-neun ilbon osaka-eseo wasseoyo

3 헨렌씨는 캐나다 밴쿠버에서 왔어요.
   hellenssi-neun caenada baenkubeo-eseo wasseoyo

4 마크씨는 호주 멜본에서 왔어요.
   makeussi-neun hoju melbon-eseo wasseoyo

5 메리씨는 프랑스 파리에서 왔어요.
   merissi-neun peurangseu pari-eseo wasseoyo

6 수진씨는 한국 부산에서 왔어요.
sujinssi-neun hanguk busan-eseo wasseoyo

7 왕밍씨는 중국 베이징에서 왔어요.
wangmingssi-neun jungguk beijing-eseo wasseoyo

8 팀씨는 영국 런던에서 왔어요.
timssi-neun yeongguk leondeon-eseo wasseoyo

Page 21: Listen and Check

1 False; **2** True; **3** True; **4** False; **5** False

Page 21: What does it mean?

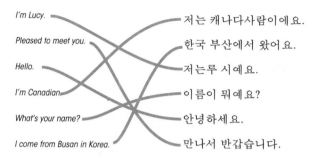

Page 22: What does it mean?

1 저는 루시예요. I'm Lucy.
2 저는 캐나다사람이에요. I'm Canadian.
3 수진씨는 한국사람이에요. Sujin is Korean.
4 이름이 뭐예요? What's your name?
5 저는 박진희예요. I'm Jinhi Park.
6 팀씨는 어디에서 왔어요? Where is Tim from?
7 팀씨는 영국에서 왔어요. Tim is from England.
8 헨렌씨는 미국에서 왔어요. Helen is from America.

Topic 3

Page 25

Check your answers with the Key Words panel on page 24.

Page 26:
Word Square

computer, sofa,
magazine, telephone,
bag, table, chair,
television

Page 26: Odd One Out

탁자 * 의자 * 소파 * 이름

한국 * 전화 * 호주 * 일본

사람 * 책 * 텔레비전 * 잡지

창문 * 수진 * 진희 * 사라

고맙습니다 * 천만에요 * 컴퓨터 * 안녕하세요

Page 28: What's this?

1e, 2b, 3f, 4c, 5a, 6d, 7h, 8g

Page 30: Who orders what?

Customer 1: green tea & rice cakes; **Customer 2:** coffee & sandwich; **Customer 3:** coffee & cake; **Customer 4:** green tea & vegetables; **Customer 5:** coffee & rice cakes

Page 31: Unscramble the conversation

g, a, e, c, f, h, d, b

Topic 4

Page 35: What does it mean?

Check your answers with the Key Words panel on page 34.

Page 35: What can you see?

침대	☑	가방	☐
의자	☑	개	☐
나무	☑	냉장고	☐
그림	☑	고양이	☑
탁자	☑	방	☑
소파	☐	컴퓨터	☑
커튼	☑	펜	☑
잡지	☐	가스레인지	☐
차	☐	책	☑

Page 37: Which word?

1 앞에 **2** 옆에 **3** 위에 **4** 위에
5 앞에 **6** 밑에 **7** 안에

Answers

Page 39: Where are the mice?

There are many possible sentences.

If you can, check yours with a native speaker.

Page 41: True or False?

1 True; 2 False; 3 False; 4 False; 5 True; 6 True; 7 False;
8 True; 9 True 10 True

Topic 5

Page 45: Can you remember?

Check your answers with the Key Words panel on page 44.

Page 46: What does it mean?

새 소파	(a) new sofa
작은 커피	(a) small coffee
작은 개	(a) small dog
낡은 차	(an) old car
큰 나무	(a) big tree
작은 쥐	(a) small mouse
큰 샌드위치	(a) big sandwich
비싼 그림	(an) expensive picture

Page 47: Listen and check

1 True; 2 False; 3 True; 4 False; 5 False

Page 47: Unscramble the sentences

1 b, c, a; 2 b, c, a; 3 a, c, b; 4 c, a, b

Page 50: Which word?

1 머리 2 다리 3 배 4 입 5 손가락 6 꼬리
7 귀 8 코 9 눈 10 팔

Page 51: At the circus

철수는 눈이 ___5___. ___1___ 가 커요.

그리고 손에 ___6___ 가방이 있어요.

순희는 코가 ___2___. ___4___ 이 작아요.

그리고 작은 ___3___ 가 있어요.

Page 52: What does it look like?

There are many possible sentences.

If you can, check yours with a native speaker.

Topic 6

Page 55: Questions and answers

은행이 어디에 있어요? ── 네, 식당 있어요.

근처에 식당 있어요? ── 공원은 학교 근처에 있어요.

근처에 호텔 있어요? ── 다리는 저기에 있어요.

공원이 어디에 있어요? ── 은행은 학교 옆에 있어요.

다리가 어디에 있어요? ── 네, 호텔은 기차역 앞에 있어요.

Page 57: Word Square

cha car/vehicle, beosen bus,
jajeon-geo bicycle, bae boat,
gicha train, taeksi taxi, bihaeng-
gi plane

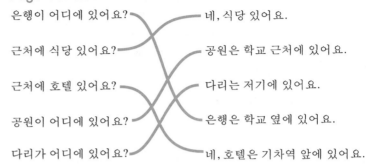

Page 60: Which way?

1 실례합니다. 버스 정거장에 어떻게 가요?
sillye-hamnida. beoseu jeong-geo-jang-e eotteoke gayo?
직진하세요. **jikjin-haseyo**

2 실례합니다. 기차역에 어떻게 가요?
sillye-hamnida. gicha-yeoge eotteoke gayo?
첫 번째 골목에서 오른쪽으로 가세요.
cheot beonjje golmo-geseo oreunjjo-geuro gaseyo

3 실례합니다. 은행에 어떻게 가요?
sillye-hamnida. eunhaenge eotteoke gayo?
첫 번째 골목에서 왼쪽으로 가세요.
cheot beonjje golmo-geseo oenjjo-geuro gaseyo

4 실례합니다. 호텔에 어떻게 가요?
sillye-hamnida. hotele eotteoke gayo?
두 번째 골목에서 오른쪽으로 가세요.
du beonjje golmo-geseo oreunjjo-geuro gaseyo

5 실례합니다. 박물관에 어떻게 가요?
sillye-hamnida. bakmulguane eotteoke gayo?
버스로 가세요. **beoseuro gaseyo**

6 실례합니다. 공항에 어떻게 가요?
sillye-hamnida. gonghange eotteoke gayo?
기차로 가세요. **gicharo gaseyo**

Page 61: Around town

These are model answers. Yours may vary slightly.

the hospital

직진하세요. 병원은 오른쪽에 있어요.

jikjin-haseyo. byeongwon-eun oreunjjoge isseoyo

the park

직진하세요. 그리고 첫 번째 골목에서 왼쪽으로 가세요. 공원은 학교 옆에 있어요.

jikjin-haseyo. geurigo cheot beonjje golmo-geseo oenjjo-geuro gaseyo.

gongwon-eun hakgyo yeope isseoyo

the bus stop

직진 하세요. 그리고 첫 번째 골목에서 왼쪽으로 가세요. 버스 정거장은 오른쪽에 있어요.

jikjin-haseyo. geurigo cheot beonjje golmo-geseo oenjjo-geuro gaseyo.

beoseu jeong-geo-jang-eun oreunjjoge isseoyo

Page 62: Unscramble the conversation

g, a, e, f, c, b, d

Page 63: Game

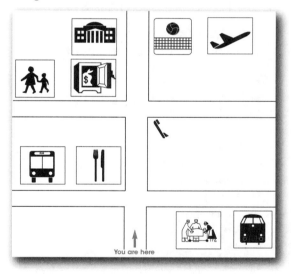

Topic 7

Page 65: What does it mean?

Check your answers with the Key Words panel on page 64.

Page 67: Family Tree

There are many possible sentences.

If you can, check yours with a native speaker.

Page 68: Family Tree

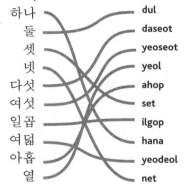

Page 68: Questions and answers

형 있어요? ─── 제 어머니 이름은 사라예요.

어머니 이름이 뭐예요? ─── 아니오, 누나 없어요.

누나 있어요? ─── 아버지 이름은 팀이에요.

형 이름이 뭐예요? ─── 저는 미국 시카고에서 왔어요.

아버지 이름이 뭐예요? ─── 저는 로버트예요.

이름이 뭐예요? ─── 형 이름은 마크예요.

어디에서 왔어요? ─── 네, 있어요.

Page 71: How many?

하나 ─── dul

둘 ─── daseot

셋 ─── yeoseot

넷 ─── yeol

다섯 ─── ahop

여섯 ─── set

일곱 ─── ilgop

여덟 ─── hana

아홉 ─── yeodeol

열 ─── net

Page 71: Korean sums

1 다섯 2 여덟 3 여섯 4 열둘 5 둘
6 열 7 둘 8 하나 9 아홉

Page 72: Family Tree

There are many possible sentences.

If you can, check yours with a native speaker.

Topic 8

Page 75: What does it mean?
Check your answers with the Key Words panel on page 74.

Page 75: The tools of the trade

Page 77: Listen and note
1 *First name:* Chanho; *Family name:* Park; *Nationality:* Korean; *Spouse:* Mikyeong Jo; *Children:* 2; *Occupation:* engineer
2 *First name:* Kelly; *Family name:* Brown; *Nationality:* American; *Spouse:* John; *Children:* none; *Occupation:* accountant

Page 78: What does it mean?
1d, 2e, 3c, 4a, 5b

Page 78: Which word?
제 __3__ 은 헤리예요. 저는 __6__ 입니다. 저는 호주 멜번에서 왔어요. 제 __1__ 이름은 저스틴이에요. 그리고 저는 __4__ 가 세 명 있어요. __2__ 한 명, 딸 __5__ 있어요.

Page 80: Word Square
factory; school; restaurant; hospital; office; theater; store; bank

병	명	처	공	장	버	니	학
원	입	틴	거	턴	있	근	교
은	뉴	가	턴	식	당	캐	요
사	무	실	는	다	는	교	멜
멜	입	인	차	주	입	극	인
택	가	자	주	에	버	장	탁
공	게	크	교	리	다	기	자
주	제	비	교	은	행	제	요

Page 81: What are they saying?
1e, 2d, 3a, 4f, 5b, 6c

Page 82: Which word?
제 이름은 김 병수 __5__ 저는 __2__ 예요. 한국 부산에서 왔어요. 저는 뉴욕에 있는 한국 식당에서 __6__ 제 __4__ 는 선생님이에요. 식당 __8__ 에 있는 아주 큰 __3__ 일 해요. 저희는 __7__ 이 두 명 있어요. 둘 다 __1__ 학생이에요.

Test Yourself

Page 84: May I have...?
1 차 주세요. **cha juseyo**; 2 녹차 주세요. **nokcha juseyo**; 3 케이크 주세요. **keikeu juseyo** 4 떡볶이 주세요. **tteokbokki juseyo**; 5 튀김 주세요. **twigim juseyo**; 6 샌드위치 주세요. **saendeuwichi juseyo**

Page 85: Listen and check
1 True; 2 False; 3 True; 4 False; 5 False; 6 False

Page 85: Which word?
저는 박 진희예요. __7__ 에 있는 __1__ 도시 인 천에서 왔어요. 저는 __8__ 예요. 영국에 있는 작은 한국학교에서 일 해요. 제 __2__ 은 의사예 요. 한국학교 옆에 있는 큰 __4__ 에서 일 해요. 저희는 __5__ 가 네 명 있어요. 아들 __3__ 그리 고 __6__ 이 세 명이에요.

Page 86: Read and check
1 True; 2 True; 3 False; 4 True; 5 False; 6 True; 7 True; 8 False

Page 87: Read and check
Check your answers with the Key Words panel on page 64.

Page 87: How do you say it?
1 제 남편은 의사예요. **je nampyeon-eun uisa-yeyo**
2 저는 여동생이 한 명 있어요. **jeo-neun yeodonsaengi han myeong isseoyo**
3 제 아들은 엔지니어예요. **je adeul-eun enjinieoyeyo**
4 진희씨 어머니는 대전에서 왔어요. **jinhi-ssi eomeoni-neun daejeon-eseo wasseoyo**
5 제 아내 이름은 클레어예요. **je anae ireum-eun keulle-eo-yeyo**
6 제 오빠는 배우예요. **je oppa-neun baeuyeyo**
7 저는 아이가 없어요. **jeo-nun aiga eopsseoyo**
8 저는 딸이 세 명이에요. **jeo-neun ttari se myeong-ieyo**

Page 88: At the tourist office
안녕히 가세요 **annyeong-hi gaseyo** *goodbye* (to s.o. leaving)
안녕히 계세요 **annyeong-hi gyeseyo** *goodbye* (to s.o. staying)
안녕하세요 **annyeong-haseyo** *hello*
고맙습니다 **gomap-seumnida** *thank you*
뒤 **dwi** *behind*
오른쪽으로 **oreunjjo-geuro** *on the right*
왼쪽으로 **oenjjo-geuro** *on the left*
버스 **beoseu** *bus*
근처 **geuncheo** *near*
큰 **keun** *big*
박물관 **bakmulguan** *museum*
어디? **eodi** *where?*

Name cards:

진희	영철	민준	수진
사라	메리	헨렌	리사
로버트	팀	켄	마크

Sentence-build cards:

이	안녕하세요	이에요	저는
씨	뭐예요	안녕히 계세요	
?	이름	안녕히 가세요	
.	고맙습니다	천만예요	

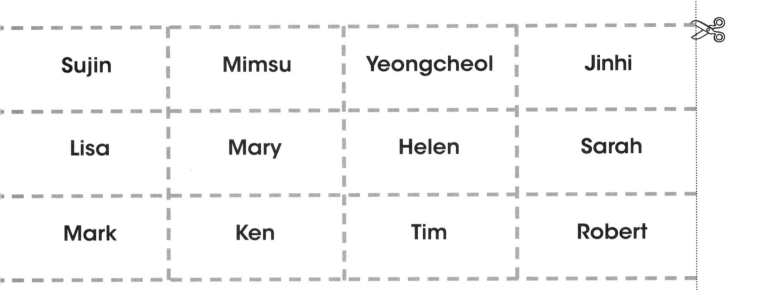

Sujin	Mimsu	Yeongcheol	Jinhi
Lisa	Mary	Helen	Sarah
Mark	Ken	Tim	Robert

I	am/are/is	hello	*(subject particle* **-i***)*
goodbye *(to someone staying)*	**what is?**	*(name title* **-ssi***)*
goodbye *(to someone leaving)*	**name**	**?**
you're welcome	**thank you**	**.**

GAME CARD ③ (see page 33)

Picture cards:

Cut-out pictures (cut round small pictures)

Sentence-build cards:

안에	위에	밑에	앞에
뒤에	옆에	없어요	있어요
고양이	없어요	에요	예요
샌드위치	침대	탁자	소파
창문	의자	텔레비전	컴퓨터
전화	그림	쥐	개
가	이	는	은

in front of	under	on/above	in(side)
there is/are	there isn't/ aren't	next to	behind
is/are *(ending in vowel)*	is/are *(ending in consonant)*	isn't/aren't	cat
sofa	table	bed	sandwich
computer	television	chair	window
dog	mouse	picture	telephone
subject particle **(-eun)**	*subject particle* **(-neun)**	*subject particle* **(-i)**	*subject particle* **(-ga)**

Picture cards:

✂

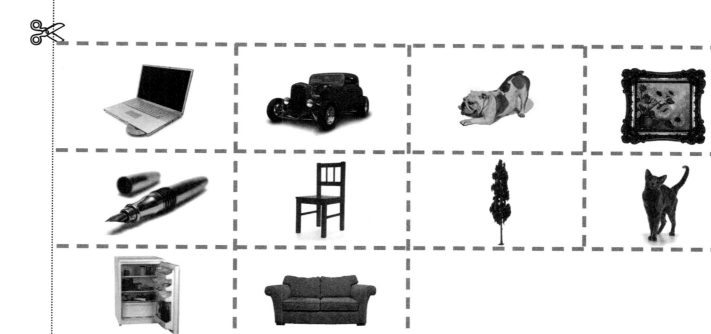

Adjective cards:

✂

큰	작은	새	낡은
비싼	싼	작은	아름다운
짧은	긴		

GAME CARD 6 (see page 63)

Picture cards:

You are here

넷	여덟	셋	열
여섯	아홉	하나	아홉
일곱	둘	넷	여덟
하나	열	넷	열

둘	여섯	넷	다섯
여덟	아홉	열	하나
넷	일곱	둘	다섯
다섯	아홉	열	아홉

1
2
3
4
5
6
7
8
9
10

Picture cards:

	(people walking)	(store)	(building)
THEATER	(fork and knife)		
($ safe)	 BUS		

Profession cards:

엔지니어	교사	점원	학생
배우	요리사	의사	회사원
회계사	운전사		